W9-BES-453

The Music Master

THE STORY OF JOHANN SEBASTIAN BACH

by
Theodore J. Kleinhans

MUHLENBERG PRESS, PHILADELPHIA

Library of Congress Catalog Card Number 62-8199

Printed in U.S.A. UB 905

Contents

1.

Folk Songs from Thuringia

FOR years the town of Eisenach had not seen so lovely a wedding as that of the banker's daughter, one balmy night in June of 1691. The blossoms of the linden trees put a touch of honey in the air, but even without the flowers it was already an evening filled with magic.

Down at the far end of the gardens, where the river flowed, the uniformed servants doled out platters of food and drink from a roast ox, a brace of pigs with apples stuck in their mouths, and a long table covered with cheeses that made one hungry just to choose. The guests strolled gaily across the lawns and among the flowers. But for some reason the party was quieter than most wedding feasts.

On the cobblestones behind the house played a little cluster of musicians. There were seven of them, ranging in age from six to twenty. Each had an extra instrument at his feet: a violin, a flute, or a trumpet. They looked and sounded like a professional band, perhaps straight from the duke's orchestra.

The youngest was a curlyheaded youngster just turned six, and, oddly, he was attracting more attention than the bride. While his brothers and sisters sawed on their strings and blew on their horns, this one stood on a herring box and sang—sang as cheerily and delightfully as a lark in the meadow.

Normally, after the guests were fed, it was time for the rustic dances. But tonight the bride said "No." This charming youngster had such a beautiful voice, she said, she just wanted to listen, and of course the other guests agreed. He sang one folk song after another, in a high clear soprano, with just a touch of roguish twinkle in his eye and laughter in his voice.

Everyone in the town of Eisenach knew that all the Bachs lived for their music. But even in a family of musicians no one expected a lad to be quite so talented, at so early an age, as six-year-old Johann Sebastian. Listening, the banker was happiest of all.

"That boy," he said to his wife, "stands out even among the Bachs. I must remember to add a few extra marks to their fee."

Like most Bachs, Johann Sebastian was born in Thuringia and, like most, he became a musician. His father and grandfather came from solid peasant stock. Centuries before, the clan had come from the rich valleys of the Carpathian Mountains in Hungary. Father, grandfather, great-grandfather, uncles, cousins, nephews—all musicians—seemed to testify that to have the name Bach was to be a musician. For miles around, the jobs with town bands and church choirs and duke's orchestras were "sewed up" by the Bachs.

Born on the first day of spring in 1685, Sebastian seemed to burst with the fervor of spring his whole life long. Though he was the baby in a family of seven, there was little time for pampering. Like the others he was expected to pull his weight.

Among his first memories was the feel of warm earth in a hill of potatoes and the waxy smoothness of an apple. But almost as early as his two wobbly legs would hold him he started fingering the strings of a fiddle and the shank of a flute. When he was five, his father gave him a half-size violin.

One of the stories his father Ambrosius told Sebastian oftenest was about great-great-grandfather Veit Bach. By trade Veit was a miller, but by preference he was a musician. All too often, his customers complained, he would let the flour spill on the floor because he was intently playing his lute.

He would play hour after hour, sometimes forgetting to turn off the great stone mill wheels. The flour sifted so thickly through the mill that old Veit had to stop and wipe it from the strings of his lute. But at least, Ambrosius said laughing, the click of the mill wheel seemed to have planted solid rhythm in the whole family, and no Bach had been able to escape it since.

From his youth Sebastian ran as free as a fawn in the forest. More than once he pulled himself hand over foot up the face of a cliff, where the mighty castle of the Wartburg stood guard over the rolling hills of the valley. He listened to the old shoemaker tell of Martin Luther, who in the disguise of a knight had taken refuge there a hundred and fifty years before. He peered out of the ramparts. He stole excited glimpses into the great hall, where the minnesingers had once staged their contests of song.

He lived surrounded by a world of music and he could not possibly have escaped. Not one of his brothers and sisters did not play, and several of them were good enough to be a real help to the family income. His father Ambrosius trained them into a family band—violins, violas, a flute, an oboe, a trumpet. Often they earned an odd groschen by performing at a county fair or funeral.

From the first, little Sebastian was the family favorite. There was a glint of blue mischief in his eye, and an overtone of innocence in his boyish soprano. Like father and grandfather before him, he learned to tuck a fiddle under his chin before most boys can lift a milk stool, and he was singing two-part harmony before most can carry a tune.

Old Ambrosius was a good man with a fiddle, one of the best, but he could teach his youngest little about singing. For that he sent him to the choir school in Eisenach where even a six-year-old was welcome if he could sit quietly and listen. Little Sebastian was the idol of the boys—too much so—and more than once they fought to see who would pair off with him in the parades and who would stand beside him.

When there was a funeral the boys sang in procession on the way to the burial ground, and often for a marriage as well, when the feast was not too late. For this there were always extra pfennigs, both for the coffers of the school and the pockets of the boys. Three or four times a week they sang carols throughout the town to bring the comfort of music to the shut-ins and invalids.

Young Bach loved his boyhood days in old Eisenach—climbing the towers of the fortress, snaring pigeons on the gables, drawing sketches of the half-timbered cottages. It was the happiest time of his life, with never care for food or family, with little to worry about but school and fun.

By his ninth birthday the family circle had begun to break up. His oldest brother Chris had gone off to Erfurt to study music with Johann Pachelbel, and a sister married and set up housekeeping. About the same time, tragedy knocked at the door of the Bach home for within the short space of nine months his father and mother both died.

The family band that had played and sung together for years scattered to the four winds. Each youngster was placed under the care of relatives and friends. As the youngest, who could benefit most from lessons in music, Sebastian moved to the home of his oldest brother Chris. It was Chris who had just finished studying under the great organist Pachelbel, and, now that he was no longer an apprentice, played the church organ at Ohrdruf.

Chris had a sound foot on the threshold of the musical world. Already, at twenty-four, many knew of his talents. He had just arrived at Ohrdruf, a pleasant little market town some thirty miles from the family home at Eisenach, deep among the firs and larches of the Thuringian Forest.

Not many young men could take over an organ and a boys' choir at the age of twenty-four. Chris had won the appointment in part because of his skill, but also because he happened to be a Bach. To learn one's trade in that period, even if it were music, one first became an apprentice, then a journeyman, and only after much training a master craftsman.

At twenty-four Chris was a master craftsman in music: organ, clavier, flute, violin, voice. Naturally he wanted to increase his income by giving private lessons. Among his many pupils, he reasoned, one might some day become famous and bring glory to his old teacher.

Whenever Sebastian told the story of his brother Chris—and it was one of his favorites—he did it with a wry twinkle. The two never really disliked each other, and yet from the first there was a bit of baiting on both sides. The trouble may have come from Chris' wife. She had been married only three or four months, and of course no bride in those first happy months of marriage likes to have a ten-year-old boy using her china and linens with typical irresponsibility.

Chris himself was a model of decorum. With his new job as *Kapellmeister* he of course had to have a wig, like the town counselors, and a plum waistcoat as well. To have all this—a new job, new clothes, a wife, a home—and suddenly to fall heir to a younger brother who was already known as something of a stubborn genius made for an eventful winter.

By the thaws of April, however, the household settled down to normal. Sebastian adjusted nicely, to both the woman of the house and the study of music. In some ways Chris was more gifted, especially at the keyboard, than his father Ambrosius had been. Month after month ten-year-old Sebastian plugged away at everything his brother set before him.

Because he himself had been taught under a strict disciplinarian, Chris insisted that the young Sebastian get a thorough grounding. There was to be no waste of time with these musical jingles that poured over the Alps from Italy and France. Good solid finger exercises and scales, with theory and harmony; that made a musician a *meister*.

When Sebastian told the story, he did not belittle his brother. He was first to admit Chris was "right in theory, even if it did not work out in practice." Everything went along swimmingly at Ohrdruf three winters in a row, with Sebastian occasionally filling in for his brother for an organ prelude.

Gradually the townsfolk began to talk about young Sebastian—how his voice trilled like a lark and how his fingers flashed over the keyboard like a hummingbird. Often they invited Chris to play for them—at a wedding perhaps, or a funeral, or a garden party. But more and more they called for young Sebastian. Finally Chris' wife suggested they take the lad around to the fairs to add a few thalers to the income.

Chris would hear nothing of the sort, and it annoyed him that she asked. Music was a gift of God, he said, not for making money but for inspiring God's people and beautifying God's service.

It was in these years that Sebastian felt his brother growing a bit strict and finally a bit jealous. Chris had taken a deep interest in his brother's training.

Each week Chris wrote an outline of what must be learned, and it gave young Sebastian little time to do what he most liked—doodle at the keyboard and elaborate on a folk tune until one could scarcely recognize it. All this, Chris told him, could come later. For now, the fundamentals were important.

In the music room there was a shelf of hand-written scores as cherished as a Bible. They were kept under lock and key and whenever some musical guest came to Ohrdruf, perhaps another student of Pachelbel whom Chris had known at Erfurt, the two would sit for hours over the clavier, working out passage after passage from the sheaf of music.

Chris seldom used them at church, perhaps because they were too flowery and elaborate. Only for a great festival would he take one to the organ and use it during the service. About the whole collection there was a certain mystery and secrecy. Sebastian used to beg Chris to allow him to play them, until they became more and more a secret challenge.

Most of them, Sebastian was told, were copies from Pachelbel—difficult, to be sure, but more than worth the learning. They were manuscript copies, transcribed from the original, and because they had never been in print they had considerable value. To see them each day locked behind the brass grill of the bookcase and to know that no one was using them seemed a crime.

For months Sebastian had been steering the conversation toward the manuscripts, and he continually pleaded with his brother to let him play them. With equal stubborness Chris said Sebastian was not yet ready, that the trills and quavers were too difficult.

Sebastian was not put off easily. Late one afternoon, when his brother was at the church, he discovered he could reach through the grill just far enough to touch the manuscripts. With his long thin fingers he could twist the rolls round and round until they were small enough to slip through the opening.

He dared not spend more than a few minutes examining the music for fear he would be interrupted, but what he saw persuaded him he must see more. Late that night, with the light of an April moon pouring through the casement, he creaked his way down the stairway past his brother's bedroom and made his way to the cabinet.

There was just enough light to see what he was doing, and in scarcely a minute he had the rolls in his hands. He catfooted once more to his room. Then, with paper and pen already laid out, he set to work. Twice before, his brother had caught him reading far into the night, and since then he had been made to go to bed without a candle.

To make out the notes by the light of the moon he

had to squint and peer. The notes were heavy fat ones, however, carefully formed, and not often did he have to stop to hold up the manuscript to better light. Page after page he copied, forgetting time and sleep. His eyes grew accustomed to the dark, and as the moon rose higher the copying went quickly.

He made some rapid calculations. From the amount of music in the cabinet he would have to work all of twenty nights to get it down. But there would be no more than three or four nights a month, at most, when the moon would be bright and the sky clear. And now that he could lay his hands on the music, he did not want to be without it.

If only he could beg or buy a candle somewhere! Or get at the manuscripts in the daytime! From a practical standpoint, he kicked himself for not thinking of it before. If he could push the table to the window, the light would be brighter. The oaken desk was heavy, and he was only thirteen, but he found he could lift one end at a time and pivot it a foot or two.

Finally he sat back on the stool and stared out over the shadows of the roof. The light was twice as good now, and he no longer felt the quivering in his eyes. Now it was not so bad trying to *read* the notes as to *write* them. The only sound was the soft scratch of pen and paper, and the rustle of a mouse somewhere in the rafters.

Suddenly a light fell across the doorsill. Chris stood there—stock-still—holding a lighted candlestick. Sebastian, facing the other way and buried in the music, still scratched away with his quill.

"Sebastian! What in the world keeps you out of bed at this time of night?" Chris strode to the table and turned his candle on the paper and Sebastian rose obediently. "So! It's the music! Haven't you heard me say a thousand times you're not to have it? Not yet, anyway. I've given *Herr* Pachelbel my solemn promise his music will never be copied by anyone, and that it will be kept under lock and key. How would you like it if you were he, and some unscrupulous publisher were to lay hands on it?

"And to think I'd never have known if you hadn't made so much noise moving the table! . . . Come now, quickly! Under the covers. That's it. Now then . . . these copies you've made." He crumpled them into a wad, lit it from his candle and tossed the burning mess onto the hearth. Briefly, the flare brightened the whole room. In another minute there was only a dull glow of ashes.

Chris tucked the precious music under his arm and stood with a hand on the door latch. "We'll speak more of this in the morning." His voice was gruff, but the glow of the candle on his face showed he was not so angry as he sounded.

2.

The Wandering Apprentice

FROM the wooded foothills of the Thuringian Forest to the heather fenlands of the Lüneburg Heide is only a hundred and fifty miles on the map. Yet nothing in the two lands is really alike—the accent, the people, the farms, or the climate. Sebastian never felt at home in the rich cities of the north, but the music he learned there surpassed anything he could have learned in Thuringia.

Even at fifteen, Sebastian's talent was so outstanding it could not be overlooked. In singing and in playing he had already learned all his brother could teach him, plus what he had learned as a choir boy. He had a solid foundation in the scriptures, and he had memorized large sections of the Psalms.

During the fourth year with his brother, a new cantor came to the gymnasium, Elias Herder. Herder was twenty-four to Sebastian's fourteen, but they had so much in common they became the best of friends. Under Herder, Sebastian became the chief descantist of the choir, and townsfolk walked for hours to the church where they could hear him sing.

No one knew better than the new teacher that Sebastian had learned all Ohrdruf could teach him. As a music master, he himself had gained his training at one of the oldest and most famed schools in the land, St. Michael's in Lüneburg. The Benedictines who were once there had founded a library of music that none could match, gathered not only from the German greats like Schütz, Crüger, Praetorius, Pachelbel, and Ahle, but also from the greats of England and France, Italy and Austria.

To be allowed to attend St. Michael's under any condition was an honor, but to be invited to sing as a matins scholar, as young Sebastian was, proved how highly Herder had recommended him to his alma mater. Sebastian set out overland, catching a ride with a farmer or hauler when he could to shorten the week's hike. The rugged villages and the rolling hills gave way to rich farms and lush pastures with windmills, and shortly before Easter of the year 1700 he arrived outside the walls of old Lüneburg.

There were thirty singers at St. Michael's. Most were

lads of Sebastian's age, though the tenor and bass were usually taken by instructors. The curriculum was largely music—clavier, organ, wind instruments, violin, singing—though nearly as much time went into Bible history, composition, rhetoric, logic, Latin, Greek, and arithmetic.

Besides St. Michael's, there was another school at Lüneburg nearly as famous. This was St. John's. The town council realized the best way to get good performances from the choirs was through competition, and each year the schools would have a "singfest" to see which could win the most applause from the crowd. Even in their singing for funerals or christenings there was a strong flavor in rivalry between the schools and sometimes the townsfolk would flock from one church to the other to hear a favorite soloist.

Sebastian did not have time to become as well known for his fine soprano at Lüneburg as at Ohrdruf. That first summer his voice began to change, and what had been a high clear soprano settled into a manly bass. But for so versatile a musician it was no real loss. He stayed with the choir as an accompanist, either with the violin or at the organ, wherever he was needed.

What made the stay at St. Michael's unusually rewarding was the great concentration of skilled musicians. One could find them on every street corner, and many of his teachers were composers in their own right. The organist at St. Michael's was Johann Löw, who had studied composition and technique in Rome and Vienna. That he was willing to spend hours with Sebastian shows how much they appreciated one another.

Another of the Thuringians there in the north like Bach and Löw was George Böhm, the organist at St. John's. Of the organs at the two schools, the one at St. John's had a far more pleasing tone and action. Through his friendship with Böhm, Sebastian had access to the best organ he had ever played.

These three often spent an evening in the coffee house together, where the talk was all of organs—the Dutch ones of Sweelinck, or the Danish ones of Buxtehude, or the German ones of Reinken. They talked of stops and of registration, of keys and of tempering, of woods and of brasses, of tones and overtones.

In one of these sessions Böhm finally persuaded Sebastian to make a trip to Hamburg. As a seaport town, Hamburg sported a bad reputation, and the townsfolk snickered a bit if you said you were going to Hamburg. All the same, it had been one of the richest cities of the Hanseatic League, and in buildings and art, trade and culture, poetry and music it had few rivals.

With Vienna and Paris, Hamburg was one of the earliest cities to organize an opera company, and the number of professional musicians there was higher than anywhere else in Germany. The more Sebastian heard about this fabulous city, especially after he had an invitation from his cousin there, the more it intrigued him. It was only thirty miles away, and he resolved not to let another week pass without making the trip.

Once he had made his first pilgrimage to Hamburg, the trip became almost monthly. The great Reinken had taken a fancy to this stripling who could so magically handle his hands and feet at the console of an organ, and he had offered to teach him. This was worth a two-day walk in anyone's ledger, especially a poor choirboy's. It was on one of these journeys that Bach met with another stroke of good luck.

The day was one of those bleak and stormy ones that often occur when the wind is off the North Sea and there is a threat of snow in the air. Sebastian had left Hamburg early, in the best of humor, but the driving wind and the hunger in his stomach robbed him of his good spirits. That was the worst thing about these trips to Hamburg—the hunger. With his cousin in Hamburg he always got good food, and at St. Michael's the same. But if he did not manage to get a ride, or if the weather was too bad to make the trip in one day, he simply had to starve once his sack of lunch had disappeared.

The wind stung more and more, and he pulled his coat around his throat. His hunger would not have been so bad were he not leaning against the wall of an inn where the rich aroma of warm pastry and sizzling duck whetted the appetite. He did not know which was worse—to be cold and hungry, or to be warmed by the inn and even hungrier.

With luck, he might catch a ride to Lüneburg with one of the travelers or wagonmen when they finished their evening meal. If not, he would have to go supperless to bed in a barn or haystack, because he could not walk all the way to St. Michael's in the dark. To keep himself cheerful and to pass the time, he sang a folksong he had learned at the knees of his mother.

A shaft of light widened into a splotch on the cobblestones, where the lanterns from the inn shed their rays.

Hardly had he turned his head toward the inn when there was a splat of something soft. There at his feet was a pair of herring, steaming. They were small, and most of the meat was gone, but at least they were something. He lifted one by the tail, and to his surprise a Danish ducat clinked to the paving. He tried the second and found a second gold piece.

He was so hungry he almost forgot to be curious. A ducat would buy a score of meals, and he lost no time going inside to order hot soup and sausage. No one would tell who had thrown him the herrings, though a barmaid lightly hinted it might have been a native Thuringian reliving his youth in the words of the folk song.

From St. Michael's he also made regular pilgrimages to the court of Duke George Wilhelm at Celle. This court mirrored the traditions of Versailles. What Sebastian loved about Celle was the chance to hear the latest French and Italian music. As a gifted performer he was always welcome, particularly for his playing of the clavier. He did not always like the music of Couperin or Raison, but its lilt and mood was something he could yearn for in his own compositions.

Even at seventeen, Sebastian's musical mind was becoming critical, like so many men of genius. He loved to be in the center of gay living and vibrant courtiers, but at the same time he thought it a waste of effort and energy. He went back regularly to Celle, and in some ways learned as much there as at Hamburg.

The French language, elegant clothes, sparkling mirrors, witty courtiers, dazzling ladies in waiting, intriguing conversation, homemade operettas—these gave him confidence. Yet he never left Celle to come back to his room at St. Michael's, to his books and his organ and his composition tablet, without a trace of sadness, a strange kind of melancholy.

Here was a part of Bach few people ever knew, except for hearsay. And yet it was so obvious in some of his music one could hardly doubt it. You feel it most keenly in the earliest songs he wrote, especially in a hymn he set to music for the organ. In it there is a touch of homesickness for the hills of Thuringia, and a respect and awe for the God who could create such beauty. Read the words and listen to the music. For an instant you will glimpse the teen-age Bach on his way home from Celle one evening at sunset:

Now rest beneath night's shadow
The woodland, field and meadow,
The world in slumber lies;
But thou, my heart, awake thee,
To prayer and song betake thee,
Let praise to thy Creator rise.

Lord Jesus, who dost love me,
Oh, spread Thy wings above me,
And shield me from alarm!
Though evil would assail me,
Thy mercy will not fail me,
I rest in Thy protecting arm.

3.

The Call of Home

SEBASTIAN spent nearly three years at Lüneburg before the call of home summoned him back to Thuringia. For several reasons he hesitated to leave. Böhm and Löw were like fathers to him, and they shared their skills generously. His trips to Hamburg and Celle he would never forget, however costly they had been in time and shoe leather.

What he longed for he could not easily put into words—the haunting sound of a shepherd's flute, or the sight of a cap of snow on a stand of firs or the homey thatch of a woodcutter's cottage. Parents he had never really known, for they had been dead longer than he remembered. But when the wind blew cold off the Atlantic, and he saw the merchants line their windows with candles and evergreen, he wished he were back among the firs of Thuringia.

Many things brought him back to the uplands he loved. For one, he was a tireless traveler and continually thought of himself as a journeyman, though already at eighteen he was a master. Long after his first grandchild was born, he still loved to find any excuse to travel —inspecting an organ, delivering a piece of music, greeting an old friend.

Unlike most musicians, he never broke his ties with his homeland, perhaps because he was never more than two hundred miles away. He never really considered a trip to Vienna or Rome, as many did. Though his contact with diplomats and royalty brought countless invitations—Poland, Russia, Sweden, France, the Lowlands —he never set foot on other than German soil.

As he grew older—and especially as he discussed his problems with Reinken, that white-haired old saint of an organist in Hamburg who always sent him home in high spirits—he knew he could not stay forever at St. Michael's. Already he equalled his teachers in his skill at the organ and, as for the organs themselves, he could not have the use of them more than a few hours a week.

Other students also had to be trained, and there were not enough hours in the day. For a time he practised "dry," without air in the bellows, when neighbors complained his pre-dawn practice drove them sleepless from their beds. The one solution was to move to a village church, where he could have an organ and a choir and a schedule all his own to arrange as he liked.

Sebastian was not yet eighteen in the winter of 1702 when he turned his face south and said good-by to Lüneburg. He had heard of an opening for an organist at the village of Sängerhausen, not far from the town of his birth. If he could win it, armed by his skill and his recommendations, he would be back in the country he wanted to make his home.

He wanted to do several things before he left St. Michael's. To leave quickly without a word of thanks to Reinken at Hamburg was hardly proper. Moreover, he had not yet been able to spend a few days at Lübeck, where that famed old organist Buxtehude was making a name for himself. Well, perhaps he could one day come back. So much for Buxtehude. For Reinken, an appreciative letter would do. Every day lost meant another risk of losing the organist's job at Sängerhausen.

During Bach's own lifetime organs and organ playing changed a great deal, with considerable thanks due to all he wrote and taught. This was a time when an organist had to be not only a performer but a composer. At the end of Bach's life, when etching a musical score became inexpensive, the poorest of musicians and the poorest of choirs could afford good collections of music.

But in Bach's youth a score was expensive. Sebastian owned only a few, and these were the gift of his older brother Chris. When Sebastian appeared in Sängerhausen on the day of the trial performance there were ten others before him, armed with rolls of music and dressed in velvet capes, trimmed mustachios, and everything else that musicians affected. Bach brought nothing, not even music, and many in the church council thought the eighteen-year-old was an apprentice, not a real contestant.

In spite of his boyish face, the council finally gave him permission to compete. One of the crusty old deacons commented that the least courtesy a young musician could show was to bring music, and not have to borrow from someone else. The young organist's reply was most polite. He asked the counselor to name his favorite chorale. "Dir, dir, Jehovah, will ich singen," was the answer.

It was a difficult request, for the song had originated only a few years before, at Halle, and was known only in a small area. Luckily Sebastian had once seen a copy at Böhm's. He seated himself at the bench and twiddled the stops. A nod to the boy at the bellows gave him a few seconds to pump the chambers full of air.

Sebastian played the melody straightforwardly, with the tune coming out not in the upper register, but on the pedals. The very expressiveness with which he played seemed to describe Jehovah as solid and dependable. The council was amazed to hear all this music from a mere boy, and was so intrigued at the flight of his fingers over the keyboard it could hardly listen to the tune that was being played.

Sebastian went to sleep that night confident he had won the post. Surely there was no doubt he had played circles around the others, and their music was hardly more than that of a shepherd with a flute compared to his. But when word finally came, he had not been appointed. The council felt the organist "should be at least a few years older than the oldest boy in the choir."

At first Bach did not know where to turn. There were cousins and brothers and uncles and aunts in every hamlet in Thuringia, and there was no danger of going hungry. But he did not like to be a beggar with all this musical talent stored within him. Neither did he like to let it lie idle. For a month he moved from town to town, visiting brothers and sisters. En route he made it a point to talk with each town organist and also the leader of the town orchestra.

By Easter his luck had turned and he was appointed a violist in the orchestra of Duke Johann Ernst of Saxe-Weimar. He really had been looking for a chance to play the music of the church, but since he could not find a vacant post he was extremely pleased with the duke's offer. It would keep him going nicely till he found what he most wanted.

To be a *Hofmusicus* or court musician was a little like being a poet laureate. It did not demand steady efforts; it was mostly an honor. Whenever the duke wanted instruction or advice in matters musical, it was to the *Hofmusicus* he turned. In the summer, when royal guests from Brussels or Paris or Vienna would visit, the court musicians wrote skits to entertain them. On the whole, official duties would take no more than a few hours a week, and Sebastian could practice and look for a church appointment to his heart's content.

What he liked best in his court position was tutoring the two small sons of the duke on the violin and the clavier. The six-year-old loved Sebastian from the start, and joked that his violin had been made by one Bach and he had been taught to play it by another. Sebastian wrote some Vivaldi transcriptions for the youngster that orchestras today still play.

Sebastian fell heir to his first organ and his first real job unexpectedly. Early one Sunday he traveled to Arnstadt to join a cousin for dinner. On the church door he noticed a placard, and he forgot all about dinner. The council sought "advice and information about the new organ, and someone to play it."

Years later Sebastian still chuckled when he talked about the organ at St. Boniface's in Arnstadt. It had cost all of two thousand gulden, which in those days was twenty year's salary. A rich burgher had donated it as a memorial for his wife, as one can still see by the inscription, or by the gold and ivory cherubs that stand above the console, holding mock trumpets.

In spite of all the fancy scrolls, it was a good organ, with twenty-six stops and two keyboards. The great organ and the swell organ were both well designed, though a bit bombastic and temperamental, in the standard lavishness of look the old organ-builder Wenden of Mühlhausen always designed into his organs. That so fine an instrument should have fallen to Sebastian, and not to an older and more experienced man, was probably due to the small size of the salary. Besides, both church and organ were so new they did not yet have a reputation.

From the moment he set fingers to the keyboard, the eighteen-year-old could call it his. The townsfolk had never heard anything so impressive, and they begged him to "not consider any other offers." There was only one problem—what to do with the former organist who had not been competent. But that proved easy. The council appointed the man honorary director of music for all the local churches, without his having to play at any.

For someone as capable and gifted as Bach to fall heir to the organ at the new church in Arnstadt was not altogether an advantage. He was only eighteen when the contract was signed, but already he was the town's social lion. Every schoolgirl had set her cap for him, and every matron with a marriageable daughter vied with all the others to invite him to her home. Imagine how difficult it must have been for a newly graduated schoolboy from St. Michael's to take the center of the stage.

Happily, his playing at the church was never burdensome, and he could finish it all in six or eight hours a week. But he disliked training the choirboys, chiefly because they were rough and insensible.

He kept up his relations with the neighboring duke, Johann Ernst, and continued as *Hofmusicus.* As close as Arnstadt and Weimar lay, with the royal court halfway between, traveling was no problem. By horse it took less than half an hour.

Almost everyone at the court talked of opera, and though Sebastian did not especially like highly dramatic music, he often wrote operettas for the court. These were given at night in the castle gardens, and they became so popular that more than one diplomat from Paris or London went home talking of the gifted young Bach of Weimar, not yet out of his teens.

Sebastian used his leisure to good advantage. His contacts with the court exposed him to a stream of music coming from outside Germany. The ducal dances and concerts and operettas gave him an opportunity to exercise his talents for writing and playing. Even so, his interest in the court did not make him forget the music of the church. He was constantly working out cantatas and dramatic skits for the boys of the choir.

Of the minor events at Arnstadt, there was one which Sebastian never forgot. His brother Jacob had been visiting him and would shortly leave for Poland, where he was determined to play in the royal orchestra. There was much camaraderie between the brothers, orphaned as they had been, and both had been trained in the household of their brother Chris. Sebastian hesitated to let Jacob go without a fitting farewell.

In great secrecy, relatives and friends from half the countryside assembled in the *Bonifaciuskirche.* Sebastian and Jacob had been out for an evening stroll. They wound up at the doors of the church, where Sebastian pretended to insist on playing a final caprice for his brother.

Without so much as a candle or lantern they made their way up the stairwell, and Sebastian took his place at the keyboard. In the shadowy pillars of the nave the voice of the organ trembled and hovered—with brilliance and melancholy, with tenderness and lightness. Jacob sat entranced at his brother's playing, and at his thoughtfulness.

Apparently he did not wonder who was pumping the bellows, so effective was the mood, until the caprice was finished. At that moment, in the church below, the crowd lighted their lanterns. As with one voice, they began to sing a reverent blessing for the departing Jacob, so softly and tenderly that many a face was stained with tears. And Sebastian at the organ played with a bird-like descant that hovered and fluttered above the solid tune of Vulpius:

Abide with every blessing,
Upon him, gracious Lord,
Bring grace and understanding
More richly through Thy Word.

Abide, thou faithful Savior,
With all thine hosts of love;
That we may all be loyal
To Thee alone, above.

4.

The Eligible Bachelor

THE townsfolk of Arnstadt did not know what to make of their gifted young organist. That he was a bachelor did not help answer their questions about him. Neither did his being so conscientious. Bach did not always do as others expected, but once he made up his mind what to do, he never delayed. And he acted as his sense of duty prompted.

Sometimes he gave the impression he was running away from work. One might even have called him temperamental, in the artistic sense, though never lazy. Perhaps his attitude toward the Arnstadters explains why.

He had settled in nicely, and what he liked best about the post was the leisure it gave. Never before had he had time to play and teach and compose the livelong day. He worked so diligently at his private composing that some of the townsfolk began to think of him as a scholar who simply pocketed the salary they paid him. He didn't enjoy drinking coffee with the other townsfolk or teaching hymns to boisterous children.

Bach was not one to belittle responsibility. He often talked of duty. At the same time, in his own mind he felt his first duty was to his art. He wanted to develop it as fully as God would allow. He did not wish to waste more time than necessary on a handful of country choirboys who needed a drill sergeant more than they needed a cantor.

Two years passed quickly from the spring he had first come to Arnstadt, and his thoughts turned to the happy days he had known at Lüneburg and the north. How good it would be to spend an evening with Böhm again! How he would love to do what he had neglected before, to study with Buxtehude for a few weeks at Lübeck. He properly requested the church council for a leave of absence and handed the keys of the organ to his cousin.

To become a rich organist it is always wise to marry the daughter of a rich organist. But seriously, in the eighteenth century by far the commonest way to fall heir to a musician's post was—marry into it!

Sebastian's trip to Lübeck was not without marriage prospects. Among young organists throughout Germany there was constant baiting about Anna Margarete of

Lübeck, the daughter of Buxtehude. Two years earlier George Friedrich Handel and Johann Mattheson had both sought the post at the *Marienkirche,* but neither had taken a fancy to Anna. She was not especially attractive, and already well into her thirties.

As for the job itself, however, there was none like it in all Germany. It paid nearly ten times what Bach was making, and at least twice that of any other organist job in the country. The instrument itself was a sheer joy to handle, with sharp action and bell-clear tones and in the best of condition.

Sebastian set out from Arnstadt in mid-November, at Martinmas. Sebastian had chosen his dates well. Music was at its peak in Lübeck shortly before the Christmas holidays. In addition to special concerts to mark the crowning of the new emperor, it was the time of the *Abendmusiken,* or evening musicales.

The *Abendmusiken* were concerts of church music which had a wide following. At Lübeck they were already generations old, and so popular they filled the church to overflowing. They were held on the last Sundays in Trinity and the first in Advent, immediately after vespers. The programs were widely printed, bound in leather as gifts for the burghers, who generously rewarded Buxtehude beyond his expenses.

Sebastian seems to have spent many a week at the home of Dietrich Buxtehude, though he probably never seriously considered marrying Anna. To begin with, she was a good sixteen years older than he. Their friendship was always a bit formal, in any case, though he enjoyed himself enough to extend his four-week stay to sixteen.

He took his time getting home to Arnstadt. It was well into February before he was back at his lodgings. The minute the townsfolk knew he had returned, the consistory formally summoned him to appear, assuming the half-comical tone villagers sometimes have. The minutes of that meeting, related in the old council book at Arnstadt, are as humorous as a book of cartoons.

Imagine the intent, wrinkled old faces around the oaken table—a retired farmer, a banker, a druggist, and two or three other cronies—taking as much interest in their twenty-two-year-old organist as if he were their son. When you read the minutes, you may not think the counselors harsh or petulant. But they do seem picayune, even a bit childish, in trying to cope with their erratic and strong-willed young genius, for they intended to "put Sebastian in his place."

First the superintendent called the meeting to order. "Tell us, if you please *Herr* Bach, where have you tarried so long. And who, pray tell, gave you permission?"

"Sir, as you know, I have been to Lübeck to study with Dr. Buxtehude. If you will recall, the council gave me permission before I left."

"That is only partially true, *Herr* Bach. I hope you will bear in mind who pays your salary. You planned to be gone four weeks. You were gone for sixteen."

"Yes, sir. But while I was gone the salary went to my cousin. Did he not fill the post to your complete satisfaction?"

"He did. But that is not the point. You were gone for more time than you had permission."

According to the minutes of the meeting, this was

not the whole of the interview. There were also complaints about Sebastian's playing, about the frills and trills in the hymns. More than once he had made the point that when two lines of a hymn carry a single thought, you should sing them straight through without a breath. For a trained singer this was excellent, but to ask a cobbler or a milkmaid to do it was too much.

There was talk also of his preludes, and how they were so long and intricate it was difficult to guess which hymn they were introducing. Sebastian, in that stubborn but polite way of his, asked the farmer councilor, "Exactly how long is too long?"

The poor old farmer couldn't tell a prelude from a chorale, but said he thought half a minute would be a good length. The others agreed. So for the next few months Bach took a sandglass to the organ with him. Never did his preludes vary by more than a few seconds from an even half minute.

Many times in the future the name Bach reappeared in the minutes of the council, none of them very important. In order to understand Sebastian's difficulties, one must have lived in a small town. The folk were trying to be helpful. They wanted to look after the welfare of the church and to help the young bachelor. But you know how youngsters are about taking advice, and oldsters about giving it . . .!

The best story of all was one an old ragpicker spread to every hearthside and inn for miles—how the organist at the *Bonifaciuskirche* was making music in church with a girl. With a girl, mind you! Naturally this was a matter the council would not dare overlook, for their wives at home were growing daily more curious.

Once more Sebastian was summoned before the council. What they charged was true. He *had* been making music in the church with a girl, he admitted. In fact, he had written the music himself. It was a sonata for organ, with a descant on the violin. The girl played the violin.

He was well aware the town fathers considered it improper for a woman to take part in a public service, even on the violin. He himself could see nothing scandalous, however. One, the girl was his cousin. Two, they were merely practising. Three, he had obtained Pastor Uthe's permission, who was present to listen. This took the wind out of the sails. It was just the kind of story he and his cousin Barbara could laugh about later.

Maria Barbara Bach was only a few months older than Sebastian. She had an appealing voice and solid training in music. Her father had been an organist too, a brother of Sebastian's father. When her parents died she had come to Arnstadt to live with an aunt.

They saw much of each other, Sebastian and Barbara. To the wives of the council it became clearer and clearer they would one day be man and wife. The only question was where and when, and of course the good women would solve that, given half a chance.

Early in the courtship Sebastian met with an unusual chance to show Barbara his varied talents. It was not with a keyboard, but with a sword. A traveling musician from Hungary was at the Bald-Headed Stag one week. He was clever on the mandolin, with a treasury of folk tunes. Many in Arnstadt went to the inn to hear him.

On the way home Sebastian and Barbara were waylaid by a gang of toughs, who sprang from the hedges and threatened them with quarterstaffs. They shouted for Sebastian to give himself up and the girl would not be hurt. The leader was a lad named Geyersbach, who played bassoon in the school orchestra.

Geyersbach's playing was only passable when he was sober, but he frequented the local taverns. More than once Sebastian had taken him to task for his faults, and this assault was the youth's way to get even. He said he would withdraw only if Sebastian made a public apology for the names he had called him before the orchestra. If not, the teacher would be beaten.

Sebastian refused, and took a step or two as if to go on. Geyersbach struck out with his stick, his eyes reddened and furious. With one sweep, and almost simultaneously, Sebastian drew his sword and flung the girl behind him. Half of Geyersbach's staff flew through the air, cloven clean by the steel.

For a second no one in the dark street realized what had happened. Then the rogues from the school, surprised to see Geyersbach still alive, grabbed him by the shoulders and beat a hasty retreat. What they now knew about their cantor did not make them play any better or sing any better, but they no longer taunted him. And, of course, to Maria Barbara, Sebastian had become a hero.

5.

The Newlyweds of Mühlhausen

IN a town like Arnstadt, with its heavy sprinkling of farmers and woodcutters and shepherds, no one doubted that Sebastian was a genius. When he first played for them as a lad of eighteen, his youth made them want to mother him. But the greater his skill became and the more his age increased, the more he grew away from the townsfolk. The Sebastian they first admired as a tow-headed stranger now appeared more and more a stubborn eccentric.

Sebastian began to look about for a spot where the

town fathers would not be quite so patronizing and where the market women would not be quite so curious when he went strolling with his fiancee. More and more he was being pressured into new work at the school, especially with the crowd of young ruffians that made up the choir. He resented this extra duty, especially because there was no mention of it in his contract.

He was twenty-two now, but he knew the older generation would continually think of him as "that boy at the *Bonifaciuskirche*" and he no longer wanted to be thought of as a boy. He got his chance just after Easter.

Forty miles away, at Mühlhausen, the organist died, and the public trial for a successor was in full swing. Sebastian had only to appear and to play and the job was his. Quickly he traveled home to assure his bride-to-be that it would not be long before they could be married. In mid-May he returned to Mühlhausen to sign the contract, but at this inopportune moment a great fire burned half the town to the ground. The church of St. Blasius was saved only by its thick walls and slate roof. The counselors were so upset by the fire that they had neither contract nor pen, so they sealed the bargain with a round of handshakes.

As soon as his term in Arnstadt was finished, Sebastian rented a house just outside Mühlhausen. He wanted to have everything ready for his bride. A distant cousin, Johann Stauber, was pastor of a village church on the outskirts, and he was a great help in the arrangements. When Maria Barbara and her aunt arrived they stayed at Stauber's in Dornheim, and it was Pastor Stauber who stood before them at the altar to marry them.

Maria Barbara was a girl of talent and spirit and she brought steadiness and orderliness into Sebastian's life. As a family man he no longer copied music by lamplight till the clock chimed two or three, and he no longer dropped ashes over his waistcoat or slept in an unmade bed.

Life would have been much harder for the newlyweds but for a sum of money that came to Sebastian through his uncle's will. It was fifty guilders, but that was nearly half a year's salary. It was more than enough to buy the furniture and linens and cutlery. Without it, he might have had to postpone the marriage.

From a standpoint of salary, Sebastian and Barbara were no better off than if they had stayed at Arnstadt. In cash he earned eighty-five guilders a year. But unlike many organists he did not get a house, though he was given a share of produce from the city's lands and forests —three bushels of wheat, two cords of firewood, six cords of kindling, and three buckets of fish. To save him further expense, the city furnished a team and wagon to haul his belongings from Arnstadt to Mühlhausen.

What the new bride and groom fancied most about Mülhausen was its legend and history. It had long been a free city of the empire, beyond the authority of any local rulers. Everything about it bore an air of glamor, from the river winding through the meadows to the spires of St. Blasius which towered overhead. For rich tapestries and stained glass, for wealthy homes and for cultured ease, Mühlhausen could outdo nearly all its neighbors.

What the brilliant young organist liked most about

the town was its organ. St. Blasius was not the chief church, but for a century its organist had been the leader of the town musicians. It was his job to direct the little world of music that had developed there.

Sebastian's organ was one of those masterpieces of the organ-builder Wenden, which are excellent instruments, even if their cases are "showy." Unfortunately this one was no longer in the best condition. Still, the skeleton was solid, and Sebastian had no trouble persuading the consistory to rebuild it.

The bellows were inadequate, especially for an organist who is skilled on the pedals. The set of bells had exciting tones, though they were not mounted near the console. The larger ranks of pipes, the *Posaune* and the bassoon, needed redoing to give a solid tone. But all this would take time, and the new organist set out to do it little by little.

Bach's duties were even lighter at St. Blasius than they had been at St. Boniface. His only real duty was to play for the Sunday services and the chief festivals of the year—Christmas, St. John's Day, Epiphany, Ash Wednesday, Good Friday, Easter, Ascension, All Saint's Day, and St. Martin's. He did not have to train a choir at all, though he was adviser to all of the choirs.

With so ideal a position, one wonders why Sebastian had reason to be discontented. But when you read his letters and listen to his stories you see the fly in the ointment. Mühlhausen was an imperial city, but it was fast losing its reputation and prosperity. Because he was not a native, the grand dames of the social circle snubbed Barbara. Since they also preferred the operatic arias from Italy to church music, Sebastian never felt really at home.

What also bothered him was an unfamiliar accent on religion, called pietism. Occasionally it went so far as to insist there was no place in the church for any kind of art—painting, sculpture, stained glass, poetry, or music. To a man like Sebastian—whose whole life was music, whose whole life was God—to suggest that music and God do not belong together is the rankest kind of heresy.

The pastor at St. Blasius was himself a Pietist, and though he was not a rabid and radical sort, Bach never felt a close relationship. Sebastian was grounded so solidly in the scriptures and in Luther's Catechism that he worried where this new pietism might lead.

What one admires most in Bach at Mühlhausen was his steadiness and sureness. Before he was married, he was often moody and withdrawn. Now when he was out of sorts, he worked out his disappointment over his writing table. But in spite of the early snubs and unpleasantries at Mühlhausen, Sebastian kept his head. Then, in the first winter of their marriage, he became the hero of the town and Barbara the most honored lady of all. For Bach composed the best cantata the city had ever heard.

Each year the city fathers were installed into office with elaborate ceremony. Traditionally the organist of St. Blasius composed a cantata. Never was it quite so striking a climax to the holidays as the year Sebastian wrote it.

The bells had been connected to the organ by then,

together with the new *Posaune* and bellows. Singers came from as far away as Dresden and, including the soloists, the size of the choir was tripled. The trumpeters played with extra flourish with Bach directing, and even the drummers seemed to sense a new spirit in the performance. "Gott ist mein König" was a cantata long remembered.

Sebastian did not need a great affair of state to set his genius in motion. Often he would write a little musical puzzle to include in a letter to a friend. Maybe it would be a fanciful version of a nursery tune for a child's birthday.

In his stay at Mühlhausen he was extremely close to Pastor Stauber, not because he was a cousin, probably, so much as for his previous kindness. Besides, Stauber was one of the few pastors in the area who was not a Pietist. The *Pfarrer* had lost his wife in death the year before, and with a large family to care for he needed help and companionship.

A big event for Sebastian and Barbara and their circle of friends was Stauber's second marriage. Barbara was bridesmaid, and the bride was none other than her aunt, who had come with Barbara when she married Sebastian eight months before. The ceremony was held in Stauber's church at Dornheim.

Sebastian searched the scriptures for a suitable text for a cantata, and he was never so in his glory as when he sat at the organ and led the singers and instrumentalists he had trained in a work of inspiration and blessing that the newlyweds would never forget.

6.

At Heaven's Gate, in Weimar

IF there was one period for Sebastian and Barbara that was happier than the rest, it was their stay in Weimar. At Arnstadt and at Mühlhausen their life had not really been complete. But at Weimar, surrounded by a host of friends and teachers and musicians and artists, they lived in their own kind of world.

They left Mühlhausen for Weimar when Sebastian was twenty-three. Duke William Ernst had hired him diplomatically both as organist and chamber musician. Officially, nothing whatever was said about the organ, for the old man who still played at the royal chapel, though seemingly not more than a few months from the threshold of death, could hardly have been replaced without hurting him. Officially, until the old organist died, Sebastian would be only a violinist in the orchestra.

Duke William was the sort of ruler whose name lives years after he is gone. He was not really peculiar or eccentric, yet he was extremely individualistic, even among royalty. He was a religious man and he felt that those not so religious as he should worship too, at the same time and in the same way as he. As a boy of six he had writen and preached his first sermon.

When he fell heir to the duchy and to the chapel, he renamed it "Heaven's Gate." He was extremely punctual and regular in morning and evening devotions. He knew nearly all of the one- or two-hundred pastors who served in his domain, and invited many of them to preach there. From time to time he visited even the tiniest of country churches. Though he seldom commented on the sermon, he was not one to keep silent if the service was so much as a minute late.

In winter, when the sun sank early, he went to bed promptly at eight, and in the summer, at nine. None of his servants or staff was allowed to stay up later than he. After the evening curfew, not a light could be seen in any of the two hundred rooms of the castle.

When Bach came to Weimar, the duke was forty-six. He had married as a young man, but his wife did not long put up with his schedules and deserted him.

Since he had no son, his heir was Duke Johann Ernst, a younger brother, and next in line was a nephew, also Johann Ernst. Johann Ernst the nephew was the duke who had taken pity on Sebastian years before, and hired him for a few months until he could find a job as an organist.

There was no love lost between the brothers William and Johann, and for years they were not even on speaking terms. The younger, Johann Ernst, was a gifted musician and composer. He had studied in Italy and was eager to develop such skill as he had. Sebastian continued to give him instruction on the violin and clavier, as he had done previously, though the reigning duke had forbidden his staff to have anything to do with his brother's court. Sebastian was not on intimate terms with the duke, who at forty-six was just twice his age. Yet they respected and admired each other. In spite of his peculiarities, Duke William was an intelligent and responsible ruler. He was one of the first to establish a universal school system, and his courts and police were efficient and honest. He was such a hard taskmaster he can hardly have had a happy personal life, yet his duchy was a model of contentment and the envy of its neighbors.

Bach's job as organist gave him ample free time. He could write and teach to his heart's content. The organ at Heaven's Gate was an extremely good one, even if it was small. With two manuals, plus a pedal and a carillon, it offered everything except volume, but there in the small chapel too much volume would have been out of place. If ever Bach wanted to use the town organ, which was considerably larger, there was no problem whatsoever, for his cousin was town organist.

His salary began at the princely rate of one hundred and fifty gulden, and during his nine-year stay at Weimar climbed to two hundred and twenty-five. There were also occasional fees from students, for testing an organ, or from a commission. Beside his work at the services, he also played from time to time with the royal orchestra.

Of the orchestra, the duke was extremely proud; it was a well trained and impressive group. On state occasions the players wore the traditional dress of Hungarian footmen, or *heyducks,* with trappings of red and black and silver that would have been an honor to any court.

Sebastian and his wife made friends in Weimar as nowhere else. As the family grew, Barbara was tied more and more to the care of the children, but invitations were unending, even in a court which retired night after night at eight o'clock.

In his first years Sebastian found a solid companion in Johann Gottfried Walther, a distant cousin who was one year older. Walther was organist at the town church of St. Peter and Paul, and a skilled performer and composer in his own sphere. As they came to know one another better and better, they served as godparents for each other's children, and wrote musical puzzles and canons to amuse themselves.

Because both retired so early, in the pattern of the duke, they often rose at the crack of dawn. A long tramp through the hills put them in fine spirits for the rest of the day, and worked up a healthy appetite for breakfast. Sometimes they came back to the Bach's for their porridge and eggs, sometimes to the Walther's. Here is a pleasant story of one of those breakfasts:

Sebastian was so skilled at sight-reading and extemporizing that one who had never seen him at the keyboard might have thought he was boastful when he frequently argued there was no piece of music he could not play on sight.

Walther always countered that however well a man plays, there are sometimes different patterns of quavers and semi-quavers which are beyond him if they occur in different patterns of the hands and feet at the same time. To clinch his argument, he said some of these are "as impossible to sight-read as to pat one's head and rub circles around one's stomach at the same time."

On this morning Bach and Walther had come in from their walk a bit earlier than usual to avoid a thunderstorm. *Frau* Walther was not yet awake, so Walther scurried about the kitchen, kindling the stove and slicing the bacon. In the next room Sebastian tinkered with some new music he found at the clavier, with Walther occasionally peeping at him through the door.

Within a few minutes Bach was sitting at the keyboard, and playing movingly through the manuscript. The notes came clear and sharp. At the rondo, however, they began to hesitate and fumble. He began again, but got no further. He tried a third time, working slowly, but broke down completely as at first. He had never been so baffled, and he did not know what to make of it.

From the doorway he heard the soft laughter of Walther, who was grinning from ear to ear. "I guess you're right, Hensel. There *is* a kind of music I can't play at sight." Walther confessed he had spent hours writing the music, making the semi-quavers move in opposite directions with each hand so it was almost a physical impossibility to coordinate the two. Years later Bach would say he had never learned so much about music as that morning he breakfasted with Walther.

Other friends at one time or another showed kindness to the young organist at Heaven's Gate. One was the head of the gymnasium, Kiesewetter, who had been a teacher at Ohrdruf while Sebastian was a student. Another, Gesner, who worked immediately under Kiesewetter, later came to Leipzig as the rector of *Thomasschule* after Bach moved there.

Of those closest to Sebastian, many more were literary men. Something mystic and religious in Sebastian's soul came close to vision and poetry, and in those days he often proofread poems for his friends. The castle's librarian was Salomo Franck, one of the better poets and hymn writers of the century. Sebastian often set one or another of his verses to music. He liked best:

> My God hath all things in His keeping,
> He is my ever loyal Friend,
> He grants me laughter after weeping,
> And all His ways in blessing end.

Bach used Franck almost exclusively for his cantata texts. To see musician and poet inspire each other was to delight in teamwork. Franck was doubtless as close to Bach as any of his friends, but others of literary fame were also close—Georg Erdmann and Christoph Lorber, to cite but two.

Sometimes Sebastian set himself to write short verse, but if the effort took more than an hour he would insist he go back where he belonged—to the keyboard.

7.

Exile in the Tower

ONE important reason that the name of Bach was so loved and admired was the attention he showed his students. Most of them lived with Bach as apprentices, and were treated as well as his own children. He gave richly of his time and experience when anyone else would have lost patience.

At Weimar, when he first began taking private students in any numbers, he had three or four under his roof. Except for his own children, he expected his students to have at least a basic skill in technique and composition before he accepted them as apprentices.

One of his Weimar pupils was Duke Johann Ernst, the ruler's nephew. With his royal blood Ernst was hardly an apprentice, since he lived at home. Martin Schubart was more typical and, like a real apprentice, when Sebastian moved from Mühlhausen to Weimar Schubart came along. He was quite gifted, learning quickly, and seven or eight years later Martin was appointed Sebastian's successor at the Chapel Royal.

There were always several Bach relatives about, sometimes living under the family roof, sometimes not. Young Bernhard Bach, Chris' son from Ohrdruf, was there. It was in appreciation that Sebastian, who had learned so much from Chris, was the teacher of his brother's son. All his students were required to maintain a library of scores, copied largely from Sebastian's. Reproducing the music in this way saved much of it from being lost.

Because his duties were not heavy, because his students could take his place, and because the duke liked to show his gifted musician as widely as possible, Bach was encouraged to travel. Almost from the start he spent eight weeks or more a year away from Weimar.

He had hardly gone from Mühlhausen when he was invited to return to dedicate the organ he had planned. He took his cousin Walther with him, and together they gave a series of concerts the townsfolk long remembered. More than one dour old counsellor, though none had shown much interest in Sebastian before, regretted he had treated him so shabbily, and he was given a handsome fee for coming.

Often the duke took his musicians to the court of a

neighboring ruler. This was the custom especially in the winter when the dukes took turns staging banquets and hunts. Bach had good cause to remember the one at Weissenfels in 1716, for the chase had gone badly and there were no boar or deer. Things were glum all around, until the duke asked Bach to cook up a musical parody of a hunt where there was drinking, gambling, and banqueting, but no game. It was the first non-religious cantata he had written and one of his best. *What Charms Me Most, the Merry Hunt,* he called it. With its clever lyrics and tuneful arias it was a great hit.

Usually Sebastian made his tours in the autumn. His fame as a consultant on organs had spread throughout Germany. When one considers how expensive travel was, it is a wonder he was invited so far, so often. From one of these trips he came back with a costly ring of opal and rubies, and he recounted its story to Barbara:

He had been invited to play at the *Hofkirche* at Kassel, and to write a report of the organ there. When he left for Kassel, neither Barbara nor Sebastian knew he would play before the crown prince of Sweden.

The prince was a good musician and had often heard the name Bach, but the cascade of music that poured from the pipes at Bach's inducement, and the sight of the feet flying from pedal to pedal so delighted him that he snatched the ring from his finger and insisted Bach wear it forever to remind him of the pleasure he had given.

Another outstanding trip was one to Dresden a year or two later. That his fame had spread to Dresden, which is a hundred miles from Weimar, is remarkable. The royal court at Dresden, however, was as steeped in music and poetry and literature as the one at Weimar. In foreign lands it was Dresden the courtiers from France and England and Italy loved best. For a musical exile from Paris to turn to Dresden was only natural; it was also a center rich with artists, and famous for its high salaries.

It was to Dresden that Louis Marchand came. He was in his early forties at the time, and had already made a huge reputation for himself at the court of Louis XIV at Versailles. Not only was he the Organist Royal but he had held six honorary posts at parishes and schools.

Marchand had a gift all his own on the clavier or organ. His boastfulness was based on sound skill, but it was also so blatant and constant that finally even King Louis himself could no longer stand it and sent him packing. Marchand scampered off to Dresden, to his friend Volumier who was directing the royal orchestra. Marchand's skill was something to hear, and at first everyone raved. Unfortunately, because his pride was nearly as loud as his playing, before long there were few he had not annoyed.

One of his favorite boasts was of the excellence of French music. It was, he said, "better than anywhere else in the world—Italian or Austrian or English or, *without a doubt, German.*" News of his chatter reached the ears of the king, who was well known for his sporting blood and for his pride in all things German. From his courtiers he sought to learn the best clavierist in all Germany, and when they suggested Bach, he dispatched a messenger. Sebastian came at once.

The project now fell to the hands of Field Marshal Fleming, a lover of music and a friend of the king. The general was instructed to arrange a musical competition. The contest plan grew to such proportions it was the major talk of the court.

The Sunday before the competition Bach played at the Chapel Royal. Marchand was in the congregation and he no doubt shared the feeling of tenseness which hung over the worshippers.

Two days later was the contest. Count Fleming had taken great pains to decorate the embassy with flowers and bunting. The hall of music began to hum with the talk of the courtiers, and by nine o'clock all seats were taken.

Bach had just passed his thirty-first birthday, and in spite of his skill he showed a trace of nervousness. The field marshal kept him company after once more checking the two claviers and finding the music in order. The judges began to grow restless. Everything was in readiness, but no Marchand had arrived.

A guest said he had heard him practising late into the night, and wondered whether he had overslept. Fleming at once sent a footman to the house in hopes of keeping the guests from further waiting. An hour passed, still no Marchand. To pass the time Bach was asked to play, and though the score was new and strange, a great deal of it Italian, his touch was sure and brilliant.

He had been playing for a quarter of an hour when the servant finally reported, breathless, that Marchand had been seen to take a seat on the morning coach to Berlin and was miles away. Fleming announced the contest finished and Bach the winner by default. He asked Bach to finish the recital.

Sebastian at length turned from the appointed music to entertain the guests with that which he had written himself—canons and fugues, mostly—and won the hearts of all. His sureness and spirit were catching. On their way home to dinner, scores of courtiers were humming the tunes they had just heard.

Those who knew Sebastian when he was still young recognized the certain magic in his music and sparkle in his personality that captured everything before him. As he grew older and his life became embittered by a hostile rector, by failing eyesight, and by noisy schoolboys, he occasionally grew peevish. But even then the old sparkle and magic regularly shone through, a bit dimmed.

Sometimes the enthusiasm of those who first came to know him made them too eager to have him for their own. When he went out to inspect an organ, often as not the townsfolk were so captivated they would stop at nothing to persuade him to resign his current position and accept theirs.

When the consistory at Halle built its new organ—a really fine instrument with few equals anywhere—the councilmen naturally asked Bach's advice, though he was sixty miles away. The post as organist was open at the time and, magnificent as the organ was, Bach would have loved to call it his own.

Sebastian liked the town and the organ so well he stayed for three weeks. In the end he knew he should return to Weimar. Yet he was so taken by the men of

Halle he composed a cantata, as a symbol of his affection and as proof of his skill.

Not many weeks after, he got a formal summons from the consistory to come and serve them as organist and *Kapellmeister*. What surprised him most were the terms The folk who had been so friendly in person had proved slave traders in the contract. It was not so much the tiny salary they offered, which was considerably less than he was earning from the duke, but the conditions they imposed.

If he were to be *Kapellmeister*, he told himself, it should be he who was to choose the music and the setting and the stops. But there in black and white the consistory told him how he was to play—accompanying the hymns with the diapason only, and perhaps one or two of the strings, but never the reeds. He was to change the stops once for each verse, no more, no less, and he was not to play preludes or descants between them.

Worst of all, he would have to give up secular music altogether. In any case, the contract insisted, the organ could not be used for anything but church music. The organist, even when he was away from church, should never belittle himself by playing secular music. He would not be allowed to take students and would remain continually in the town with no outside engagements.

To be an organist at Halle would be to live in a strait-jacket, and it is little wonder Bach refused in spite of the magnificent organ. At first the Halle council called him all sorts of blackguard and said he had shown interest in the position only to win himself a raise from the duke. Actually, one of the big factors in his decision was his growing family and his need to care for their education, which he could hardly have done on the tiny income at Halle.

Fortunately the ill feeling was soon forgotten. Several years afterward Bach was invited to inspect the organ once again, and to give a concert. It was a week-long celebration, with a heavy fee and heavy food, and he felt like a king at their hospitality. At the final banquet the menu alone was proof of their respect—a roast ox, spiced and fatted; pike in wine sauce; tureens of steaming veal and mutton; hot cured ham; pumpkin, squash, peas, potatoes, carrots, and beans; fried biscuits; an appetizer of hot buttered asparagus; lettuce, radishes, candied orange peel, and preserved cherries.

All the while he was at Weimar Bach was supremely happy. His family grew yearly and he found in Barbara a loving spouse and a dutiful mother. Like most Germans he had an almost insatiable desire to travel, especially while he was young. What he loved at Weimar was his constant opportunity to see new towns and to meet new acquaintances.

In some ways Bach was a true son of the great missionary of the Germans—Boniface. In any case the two certainly believed in the same motto—*timor dei, amor peregrinationis*—"the fear of God and the love of travel." And so long as the duke encouraged Sebastian to travel, to give concerts, to test organs, he did not mind turning out the lights with the birds nor object to the other peculiarities of the duke.

Little has been said here about one of the musicians at Heaven's Gate who knew Bach well—Johann Samuel

Drese. He was a competent *Kapellmeister,* and he gave his young organist a free hand in all things musical. But Drese aged quickly, in mind and spirit, and he was already an old man at sixty-four when the twenty-three-year-old Bach arrived. Almost from the first Sebastian carried much of the old man's load, especially in the writing of cantatas.

Drese died in 1716, when Bach was an experienced thirty-one. Since Sebastian had been doing the *Kapellmeister's* job for years he naturally expected the post to be his. But the duke was not altogether satisfied, largely because Sebastian had refused to give up his forbidden ties with the duke's brother.

First the duke sought to hire the well known organist Telemann. When that failed he appointed the son of Drese, who was a run-of-the-mill musician. Sebastian was extremely angry and vowed he would leave Weimar at the first opportunity. The duke tried to mollify him, raising his salary and encouraging him to stay. But Sebastian, once his mind was set, was not to be mollified.

Earlier that year he had met Prince Leopold of Cöthen, a charming young man with much musical talent. When Leopold heard of Bach's dissatisfaction he at once offered him a post at Cöthen, and Bach leaped to the bait. He immediately asked permission to leave the duke's service.

The duke was in a bad mood and did not like the thought of losing so good an organist. He ordered Sebastian to give up all thought of going to Cöthen. What made him especially angry was Bach's dallying with a noble family he hated, when he had given strict orders there was to be no fraternizing. But Bach was as stubborn as the duke.

Tempers flared so hotly that the duke clapped his organist into the castle tower and put him under armed guard. He did not prevent Barbara or the children from seeing him, but swore Sebastian would not leave until he became more humble.

In one way the month of house arrest was the greatest month of Sebastian's life. In his tower overlooking the valley he had every comfort except freedom—a blazing fire, a soft bed, tasty food, a good clavier, and reams of paper and ink. For once he could put down into writing the wonderful music he was continually playing.

The book that came from his quill during that rain-soaked November was the *Orgelbüchlein—The Little Organ Book*. Its every mood and nuance was in the dedication he wrote on the title page:

> To honor God alone Most High,
> And train my neighbor too thereby.

Long into the night and early in the morning the lamp shone from the tower, far beyond the required curfew of eight when the castle should have fallen dark. Sebastian wanted to salvage what he had learned in those rich years at Weimar, by writing it down both for the training of others and the worship of the Lord.

He began by choosing a hymn for each Sunday of the church year, and then set about to compose the preludes. Many proved to be far more elaborate than a mere prelude—*fantasia* would be a better word. To disguise the melody and build up an independent piece of music was his first intent, so the hymn would fall more freshly on the ears of the congregation.

When Bach was alone with his God and his music, it is difficult for anyone to fathom the depth of his devotion. Still, the *Orgelbüchlein* is a good insight, for it shows the splendor and completeness of the life of a child of God—a life that is filled with trust, joy, dread, and peace. All these, in a splendid variety of musical patterns and keys, one can feel in Bach's music; it seems a window into the soul.

The words of many of the old chorales were a comfort to him in the tower, as they were all the days of his life. Two of Sebastian's special favorites were these:

> The old year now hath passed away;
> We thank Thee, O our God, today
> That Thou hast kept us through the year
> When danger and distress were near.
>
> Jesus, Sun of life, my splendor,
> Jesus, Thou my friend most tender,
> Jesus, Joy of my desiring,
> Fount of life, my soul inspiring.

The Bach who lost himself in his music that month was a truly magnificent genius. Everyone soon forgot the squabble which put him under arrest. The jokes and gossip of the courtiers persuaded the touchy duke he could not hold his organist forever.

But so long as the world lives no one will forget the music that was written there, for it is still the voice of trust and faith, speaking of a hell of darkness and a heaven of light.

8.

The Hofmusicus of Cöthen

WITH its scrapings and bowings, its "Your Excellencies" and "Your Graces," a royal court can be as deadly as a viper. It can kill both body and soul. It can also be a source of inspiration, a challenge to the mind and the imagination.

When Bach became court musician at the duchy of Cöthen, Prince Leopold was a young man of twenty-three, and Bach thirty-two. In many ways the relation was that of tutor and student, or father and son, rather than musician and prince. Though the court had drawbacks, by location and atmosphere and size, the six years

Sebastian spent there were among the pleasantest of his life.

The young prince was a bachelor, as gay and spontaneous as any. He had traveled throughout Europe, and his love for music was deep and genuine. Though his duchy was small and no longer well to do, his castle was first-rate, a showpiece of Thuringia. A wing of this castle sheltered Sebastian and his family for six years.

Though his lands and income were small, Leopold supported a court band twice the usual size. There were eighteen players. Some of them doubled in other jobs—footman, librarian, tutor. The prince spent up to one-fifth of his income on the orchestra, and never stinted the purchase of instruments or music.

The band's official title was "The College of Music." It rehearsed regularly in the wing of the castle where Bach lived, and often the prince himself took part. On the violin and clavier he was gifted, though he started late in life.

In only one respect did Bach feel that Cöthen was lacking in the field of music for the church. Ever since the Reformation the duchy had been of the Reformed faith, with the worst restrictions of life and spirit a too-strict Calvinism sometimes produces. In church, for example, there could be no choirs, and no preludes or hymns.

These were considered too elaborate and sensuous for the worship of God, and were relegated to beer halls and dances. Any singing in the church had to be a simple solo, unadorned, preferably with a lyric from the Psalms.

Bach did not like so strenuous an atmosphere, and years later when he returned to Cöthen from Leipzig he occasionally brought a choir with him to show the townsfolk how delightful and inspiring the public praise of God could be. Neither at the castle nor in the town was there a really good organ, though both were passable enough to keep his skill from growing rusty.

Hardly had he settled his wife and babies into the new quarters at the castle when he was off on another inspection. This time it was to Leipzig and the new organ of the university church. He had played there several times, on the invitation of Johann Kuhnau. Kuhnau was the cantor of the *Thomasschule* and a close friend of Sebastian, often serving him when an organ was dedicated.

As a bachelor the prince was a lover of the arts, and a man who liked good companions. He seldom went anywhere without Bach, and frequently three or four others also. Sometimes the trips were to concerts or hunts, sometimes to shoots or parties. One custom of the day was to take the mineral baths at a spa, enjoying the music and culture that gathers at such a resort. The prince loved to visit such places as Kassel and Carlsbad.

It was after such a trip to Carlsbad, in the mountains of Czechoslovakia, that Bach was returning home loaded with gifts for his wife and children. A servant had run ahead to tell him the awful news. Barbara was dead. Stricken suddenly, she had been buried, and the children placed in the care of a maid. The blow was a shattering one, even for the man who had grown up an orphan and had seen death so close and so often. It was a possibility he had not even dreamed of. In the melancholy hours when he was alone with his thoughts, he found much comfort in hymns.

One of these he wrote in a music book for his son, after his wife's death. It is testimony to his courage:

> If you but suffer God to guide you
> And hope in him through all your ways,
> He'll give you strength, what e'er betide you,
> And bear you through the evil days.
> Trust God, and his all-loving hand,
> And build your faith on more than sand.

Sebastian had always been extremely close to his children, and the loss of his wife drew him even closer. The couple had brought seven babies into the world, but the ravages of plague and smallpox and pneumonia had claimed the lives of three almost before they were out of the cradle. Dorothea, twelve, was now nearly old enough to play at being a mother, and Friedemann, the darling of his father, was ten. Emmanuel was seven, and Bernhard, five.

For more than a year the Bach household ran smoothly, with a maid to care for the cooking and cleaning. But month after month Sebastian missed the mother's touch in the training of the children. Because of his obligations to the duke and his trips away from home, he could scarcely fill the shoes of both mother and father.

One of the soloists in the town was a girl of unusual voice, Anna Magdalena Wilcken. She had come to the court two years earlier, scarcely out of pigtails, and had won the hearts of all. Even the tots who played on the duke's lawn where jousts had once been held knew her affectionately as Lenchen, and more than once she had cared for the Bach children while their parents were at a dinner or a concert.

She came from a family absorbed with music. Her father was the trumpeter at the court of Weissenfels, and had once taken part in a cantata Sebastian wrote there. Lenchen had a clear and pleasing soprano, and was trained at the clavier and the violin. In fact, she had come to Cöthen at the request of the prince, as a salaried musician, and when she first came there was some talk she would be his bride.

To be near Lenchen was a pure delight, and the more he thought of her, not only as a bride but as a mother for the children, the more Sebastian wanted her. He hesitated only because of her age. She was scarcely twenty, and he thirty-six. She must have sensed something in his hesitancy, and encouraged him by her kindness to the children. Finally he asked her to be his wife.

The marriage was set early in Advent in 1721, about a year and a half after the death of Barbara. The prince himself blessed the wedding with his presence. Sebastian, as he loved to do for any occasion of importance, wrote a poem for the event, which he afterward recorded in an album. Like his music it gives a good glimpse into the tender feelings he henceforth had for her:

> Your servant, worthy bride of mine!
> May happiness attend you.
> Whoever sees your wedding garb
> And wreath and laurel 'round you
> Must smile within in purest joy
> And wish you every blessing.
> What wonder I, with heart and lips,
> O'erflow with joy to greet you.

A week after Sebastian married, Prince Leopold also took a wife. His bride was lighthearted and flippant, though pleasant enough on the surface. The prince's marriage changed the pattern of the court. The new princess resented the strong attachment that had taken root between her husband and his *Kapellmeister,* not only because one was royal and one a commoner, but because her husband spent more time and money on the band than on her. From the outset she began to wean Leopold from his music, and from Sebastian.

During the past year or two Bach had begun to tire of Cöthen, and quite probably what kept him on was the death of his wife and the concern for his children. Within a year, however, he did make a famous trip to Hamburg, the city whose name conjured visions of great organs and magnificent music.

It was at Hamburg, of course, that he had always been so welcome as a boy, when a student at Lüneburg. He never thought of the four manual organ there and of the great Reinken without remembering the footsore trips and the time he would have starved but for the kindness of the unknown traveler who threw him golden ducats stuffed in the head of a herring.

Reinken was the grand old man of German music. The last time Sebastian had seen him he was seventy-eight, and now he was a still active and alert patriarch of nearly a hundred. He still handled the organ at the *Katharinenkirche* better than any of his contemporaries, and his list of students and admirers was the envy of all Germany.

Reinken had a soft spot for Bach. When Bach arrived in Hamburg, Reinken not only listened to him play but invited other organists and three of the town fathers. For hours Bach played for them, his hands roaming skillfully over the manuals and his feet, more dextrous than Reinken's, playing a two-part fugue on the pedals.

As the highpoint of the little concert he had chosen the chorale *By the Waters of Babylon.* Reinken had once written a fugue and fantasia on this theme, which was regularly used as a test piece when an organist competed for an audition. That Sebastian should choose this delighted the old man.

Bach's conception of the hymn was so vast and so intricate that even Reinken gasped. As the music flowed out over the rafters of the church it was apparent that this was no mere prelude, nor even a fantasia or fugue. This had not been done before; it was like a symphony on the organ with the various themes developed and restated from key to key and from stop to stop.

The organ rang with pleasure for a long half hour. Finally the music ceased. With his eyes shining, and his hand unsteady, Reinken took Bach by the shoulder. His voice quavered with emotion. "I had long thought this art was dead," he confided, "but in you I see it still lives."

Of the two great organs in Hamburg, the *Katharinenkirche's* and the *Jacobikirche's,* the latter was without an organist. Reinken strongly recommended Bach, and of course Sebastian would like nothing better. He applied for the post and, on so strong a reference, had high hopes of winning it. But the competition was not yet scheduled, and he could not be absent too long from Cöthen. The committeemen were so excited by his playing however, that they waived the requirement for meeting the test.

Bach also had the opportunity to meet the pastor of the *Jacobikirche,* Erdmann Neumeister. Neumeister was a gifted poet, and Bach had previously used his texts for cantatas. The more he dreamed of the four manual organ and the more he dreamed of a team of poet and composer, the more he wanted to live the rest of his life at Hamburg. The university was there for his lectures, the opera for his tunes, and the gymnasium for his sons.

On the trip back to Cöthen his head was full of dreams and he counted his days in Thuringia as numbered. When a letter finally came, however, it was not a summons to Hamburg. Instead it was a brief report that another had won the post. He was at first terribly downcast, though later, when he heard the full story from Neumeister, it brought a grin.

The organist who won the position, as one of the critics wrote, could play far better with his money than with his fingers. He had made a gift of more than four thousand marks to the council, and been appointed out of sheer gratitude.

What little revenge there was came in a sermon Neumeister preached the following Christmas. He told the gospel story of the hosts of angels who sang their hallelujahs at Christ's birth. If one of those angels from Bethlehem were to come to the *Jacobikirche,* said Neumeister, he would have to fly home again if he had no money, for the council would turn him out.

Back in Cöthen Sebastian helped raise his household

of children. The girls were not to be overlooked either, he would say, for they would one day be wives and mothers. Even if they were not professional musicians, how could they help their husbands and be intelligent and love music if they lacked an education?

The oldest of the boys was Friedemann, on whom Sebastian showered every attention. His father expected much of the lad; he was under continual strain. But Friedmann was so high-strung and emotional his father never ceased to worry.

Once, when Sebastian caught Friedy in a lie, he became so angry he would not speak to him for days. To say "I'm sorry" was as hard for the young fellow as it must have been for the prodigal son. But when Friedy did apologize, Sebastian hugged him nearly to death.

At ten Friedy got his own music book. Sebastian wrote it out with his own hand, and gave a great deal of the instruction himself. First he composed a series of scales, marking off the fingering. At the top he marked *"applicatio."* Even so simple a book as the *Clavier Book* was tinged with Sebastian's love for God, and he wrote the same initials at the top which appear on most of his music—INJ (*in nomine Jesu*—"in the name of Jesus").

Wherever you look in Bach's music you find trust and faith. Usually they are so much a part of him, woven into the music and the text, that one is apt to overlook them. He was also fond of marking his sheets with J.J. (*Jesu, juva*—"Jesus, help me") as a prayer for inspiration. And at the end there was often an S. D. G. (*soli deo gloria*—"to God alone the glory") as a thanks for what he had been given the strength to write.

Sebastian almost singlehandedly invented a new kind of fingering. Before his time, few organists would have thought of playing with the thumb or with the ring finger. Sebastian changed all that. He usually combined his exercises for Friedy with an interesting story, as when he taught the scales. Here he told the story of the Latin psalm, and explained how the different tones for do-re-me came from the words *"Dominus regit me."*

The *Clavier Book,* which he began as a workbook for his son, later became the foundation of the *Well Tempered Clavichord.* Tempering is a bit of musical history the passage of time has masked, and it is forgotten by all but the scholars.

The problem of keying and pitching an instrument was difficult. It was Bach who sat down with a pencil and paper and worked out how the strings and horns and the organ and the human voice could be made to harmonize. To oversimplify, imagine a keyboard with only the white keys before anyone has discovered the black. Think how difficult it would be to play or to compose without the sharps and flats!

In this aura of instruction his wife Lenchen did not escape. At twenty she was in some ways as much a student as a wife. She already had some skill at the clavier, which was unusual for a woman, and the marriage was less than a year old when Sebastian presented her with a *Clavier Book.* The tunes were somewhat simpler than those for Friedemann, but in this, as in a book he wrote for her several years later, were many words of devotion and poetry composed by an admiring husband.

In the book were several solos she might sing, and

countless little sarabands and *gigues* and *bourrees* and chaconnes she might play. They had been passing little jokes between them about the importance of music in the church, in spite of what the Reformed preacher insisted. Sebastian jokingly inscribed the booklet as if it were a doctor's prescription. "Against Calvinism!" Surely so pure and lilting a remedy was a good cure.

From its perch in the castle the music room overlooked all the valley. When Sebastian sat and looked down over the village, where smoke curled from the cottages and where the herdsmen tended their lambs, he often grew philosophical. Then he would write a homey poem for his wife, and leave it at the clavier as a surprise. One of the cleverest of these is about his pipe.

As soon as I have filled my pipe
With costliest tobacco
And light it up to pass the time,
The smoke swirls round with doleful voice
And states in clearest diction
That I am also fiction.

My pipe is made of clay and earth,
That I alike am made of.
And I must one day turn to dust,
A pipe that breaks and crumbles.
As clay that's gone in twinkling flash
My fate alike dissolves to ash.

Such noble thoughts swirl through my brain
With every puff and gurgle,
And so I smoke in peace and ease
And build my dreams just as I please.
No matter where I chance to be,
This little pipe, it teaches me.

All his life he had a warm spot for children, whether they were his own or someone else's. He and the prince regularly stood godparent for each other's babies, and for one of these christenings he composed a "darling bit of music" to the new princeling.

He hesitated to play it, he has written, for fear of waking the little chap in his crib, but the mother might use it as a lullaby. "A baby's hearty crying," he goes on, "is not a complaint against the evil of the world, but a chorus of joy at being alive.'

These were the touches that made Sebastian lovable. Little wonder that Prince Leopold made him his honorary *Kapellmeister* for life! For all the birthdays in the royal family and all the anniversaries Sebastian would compose a musical ode. These became so popular he often won commissions to write them for other nobility.

This is how the *Brandenburg Concerto* came to be written: The Margrave of Brandenburg had been a visitor to the court and was so taken by the young artist he commissioned a set of concertos for his capelle. Bach had never composed for quite so large a group of players before, nor in a form so symphonic.

There was a large bonus for Sebastian when the works were finally finished and it was well earned. The instruments kept up a merry banter from section to section, like two great flocks of magpies arguing about who owns the rookery. The Margrave made the manuscripts a part of his library. Another copy found its way into the scores of Leopold, where the music could often be heard on a summer's evening, echoing lightheartedly through the great keep of the castle.

9.

The Cantor of Leipzig

EVEN before he left the court of Cöthen, Sebastian was no stranger to Leipzig. The cantor at St. Thomas' had been Johann Kuhnau, who often invited him to visit and to perform on the organs. Kuhnau was an old man, but he had extraordinary talent. If he had not been broken by the pettiness of the council, he might well have been as great as Sebastian.

Both for his performing and his composing Bach also was a name to conjure with in Leipzig. He had performed half a dozen cantatas there, as well as the *St. John Passion*. Townsfolk and students had grown accustomed to good music, and now that Kuhnau was aged and feeble they often commissioned special works to fill the gap.

At first there was considerable haggling about a replacement for Kuhnau. He had been a mild and obedient organist who lived only for his music. Now the council was eager to get a man of talent but also a man who would take orders, who would do as he was told.

They first thought of George Telemann, who had once spent a year at the university church in Leipzig. The cantatas he wrote had been the talk of the town, and the students were equally enthusiastic. Telemann had been in the north so long, however, that he felt it was home, and the call to Leipzig served no purpose except to raise his salary where he was.

The next choice was Christoph Graupner, the *Kapellmeister* of Darmstadt. Graupner was cagier than Telemann had been, for he showed an interest in the job and composed a cantata. The court which he served, Electoral Hesse, was one of the richest in all Germany, and the landgrave knew a good *Kapellmeister* when he saw one. Graupner was offered a gift of four or five years' salary, and a pension for wife and children, provided he stayed at Darmstadt. He stayed.

The counselors at Leipzig were not happy about Graupner's refusal, but they had to call someone. They called Bach. One cannot shoot at the moon, they said, if one knows the bullet will not carry so far. And Bach could not be so bad, for was he not the man who had composed the *St. John Passion,* which was still the talk of the intellectuals?

When Lenchen and Sebastian decided to pack their belongings and come to Leipzig, the job was not the sole reason. For one who had been a *Kapellmeister* at a royal court, even a small court, to become an ordinary cantor, or teacher of music, was a long step down. They discussed it long, but finally the choice was for Leipzig.

For one thing, Sebastian felt his real calling in the church, and he was never so happy as when his music could serve God. For another, he was always a bit cramped by the atmosphere of Calvinism at Cöthen. To be back among Lutherans would be a pleasant homecoming. Not least was the security the new job could bring, not only for him but especially for his sons. They were nearly ready for the gymnasium and, in a few years, for the university. For his sons, no price was too high.

Prince Leopold would miss his *Kapellmeister,* but he wished him godspeed. Leopold knew that his marriage had changed their lives, and both were now going their own way. But the prince did not forget the man who had taught him so much of music and of the world, for he made him honorary *Kapellmeister*. From time to time he would invite the Bach's to return for a visit, including a generous gift for traveling expenses.

To be cantor of St. Thomas one needed many skills, and not least of these was diplomacy. The head of the school was the rector; the second in command was the co-rector; the third was the cantor. In a school founded to teach music, it was odd not to have a musician in charge, as Bach was soon to learn. But for a year or two, in the busy excitement of Leipzig and the stimulation of his talents, he thought life could not be pleasanter.

From the first it was obvious he would not have a free hand. The list of duties which he swore to perform when he took the oath of office was extremely restrictive, but not many thirty-eight-year-olds, especially when they are so open-minded and optimistic as Bach, would have interpreted them in their narrow meaning.

In his contract he promised to teach diligently, to lead a blameless life, to set a good example, to show respect and obedience to the council. He was not to let the boys sing outside Leipzig without the consent of the council. If a counselor wanted them at his home, he was to oblige immediately. He was to teach the boys on all instruments, to save the expense of hiring players.

Such music as he wrote or played was to be devotional, and neither operatic nor lengthy. The boys were to be treated kindly, and if strong punishment were required, he was to report it to the council. He was also required to teach four hours of Latin, though, if he preferred, he might hire a substitute. He was not to leave the city without the permission of the burgomaster. He was to chaperon the boys when they sang at a wedding or funeral, marching with them in the streets. He was to accept no office in the university.

The *Thomasschule* was a school founded by the Augustinians more than five hundred years before. At the time of the Reformation it was one of the best in Germany, and its rector became a firm adherent of the new faith. As a master musician and a teacher of musicians, he liked best what Luther was saying about music for the church—"The devil must not keep all the good tunes to himself!"

Though St. Thomas' always maintained a high standard of music, the buildings themselves, with their sagging gables and leaking eaves, were sadly neglected. When Bach arrived, the rector was more than seventy years old. For years he had had no interest in anything but his salary. He could control neither students nor teachers, and the classrooms had become such a circus no one who could afford to send his sons elsewhere kept them at the *Thomasschule*.

St. Thomas' took students when they reached ten or eleven, and taught them for six years. If a student was especially gifted he might stay a few years longer, as Bach had done at Lüneburg. Fifty-five of the boys were boarding students, from the farms and villages around Leipzig, and that many more were town boys, spending their nights at home.

As one of the three important members of the staff, Sebastian had his quarters right in school. The rooms lay beside the River Pleisse, and across the way one could see the quaint old church, with its turrets, courtyard and fountain. When Sebastian and Lenchen arrived, they were assigned ten or eleven smallish rooms. As the family increased he got more space.

There were many exciting hours among Bach's first days in Leipzig. Even before he had taken the oath he had given a cantata, and as far away as Hohenheida and Markkleeberg the villagers were talking of the new cantor. Among the women of the market, who were quickest to gossip, some thought his music like a choir of angels. Others argued he was bringing comic opera to the very altars of God.

10.

The Lay of the Land

TO anyone but Johann Sebastian Bach, to be the director of music for four churches but to be the organist at none would have been a baffling job. But this was precisely the work of the cantor. Historically, the post had grown until it included not only teaching music to the boys of St. Thomas, but taking charge of all things musical at the four churches.

Oldest and largest of the Leipzig parishes were the *Thomaskirche* and the *Nicolaikirche,* which had a healthy and natural rivalry. The *Petruskirche* boasted neither the fame nor the age of the others. And the

Neukirche, as the university church, tried to hold its independence.

The first task of the cantor was to provide music for the churches of St. Thomas and St. Nicholas. He was to train the players and singers, to direct the work of the organists, to choose the anthems, and to provide general advice and control over all music in any way connected with the church.

The service in Bach's day was long and elaborate. The chief service was the Communion, celebrated each Sunday morning. Each Sunday afternoon came the vespers. The order of worship began officially at seven in the morning, when the ceremonial candles were lit and carried to the altar, the Leipzig church bells having already begun their pealing at six.

While the congregation assembled there was a long prelude on the organ or, at festivals, on a violin, oboe, or viola. Often the boys sang a motet as well, with a solo and a chorus and a recitative, to set the mood for the service.

When the pastor read or chanted the introit, the first scriptural reading of the service, the choir sang the Kyrie, or the "Lord Have Mercy." Sebastian liked a great deal of variety in the Kyrie and thought it only fitting the congregation should also ask for forgiveness, with their own voices. Often he had them sing this in the form of an anthem, "Kyrie Gott Vater in Ewigkeit."

For the Gloria he also replaced the choir with the congregation on many occasions, and had them sing "Allein Gott in der Höh sei Ehr!" Then there was the prayer and the epistle, sometimes sung, sometimes read, and the chorale by the congregation. The gospel came next and, by old custom, on feast days it was chanted by two pastors, one taking the direct quotes of Christ and the other the evangelist's part, singing different pitches.

The Creed was read, chanted, or sung in several forms and if all joined their voices in the hymn "Wir glauben all' an einen Gott," the organist usually worked in a few flourishes for variety. From the musician's point of view, the cantata that followed and immediately preceded the sermon was the high-point of the service.

A cantata was a kind of musical sermon, lasting about twenty minutes. It contained solos, duets, trios, choruses, arias, recitatives, chorales, even instrumental quartets, if the composer felt they fitted the mood of the text. Next came the sermon, which lasted an hour, followed by an organ voluntary, the prayers, and the benediction. The hymns and the liturgies of the Communion, with much singing during the distribution of the bread and wine, concluded the service.

This was a long and complex order. No wonder the choirboys sometimes failed to sit patiently for three or four hours! In winter, when the co-rector pronounced the church too cold for the younger boys, they left the unheated church for the hour of the sermon, sitting before a blazing fire at the school. But even there one of them was appointed to read the sermon aloud.

That one or another of them used to sneak away after the roll was taken is not surprising. To sit so long on a cold hard bench when one is scarcely twelve is bound to produce mischief—like throwing paper wads or sailing paper airplanes or noisily munching nuts.

The boys sang not only for the three hour service in the morning, but for midafternoon vespers as well. From the short prayer service at noon they were excused, for that was the only time they might eat their dinner. In vespers there was only a small amount of choir music, usually a motet, but they were not totally free until nearly sundown. By then it was bedtime.

To write the music for the service was not nearly so difficult as to rehearse it. One or another of the boys was always ill, or at home, or his voice had changed, or he had a cold, and always there was much shuffling. Of all of the boys in the schools, more than half were not available, either because they were too young and their voices were not yet sufficiently trained, or because they were too old and their voices *had* changed!

The larger of the choirs numbered twelve to sixteen boys. Each Sunday it alternated between St. Thomas and St. Nicholas. The smaller choir was usually eight, depending on how many were needed to play instruments and how many went to the New Church or to St. Peter's. To sing an ode or a passion on some important festival, Bach could scrape up a total of twenty-five or thirty, counting six or seven of the Thomaners in the band and another eight or ten who were hired by the city.

One Sunday the main cantata would be at St. Thomas', and the next at St. Nicholas'. When there was no cantata, there was at least a motet. On great days like Easter or Christmas, however, there must be a cantata at both churches for both services, and this was arranged by having each choir learn a cantata, but sing it in the morning at one church and in the afternoon at the other.

When one considers there was not only a Christmas but also a second and third Christmas, and that there had to be two cantatas for each, one can see how busy Bach was writing out all the parts and rehearsing the lines. Since he naturally could not direct two choirs at two churches, his oldest student or prefect would help. Occasionally, since the churches were not far distant, he could fly from one to the other and direct both.

All this sounds as if Sebastian did not have a second he could call his own, nor an hour to spend with his family. Still, the cantatas were so much his pride and joy he loved the time he spent on them. For five years he composed at least one for each Sunday, taking as much care as if he were composing an ode for the death of a queen.

His schedule of teaching slackened off, once he had hired a tutor to substitute for him. He still had to keep an eye on the young man, who was teaching not only Latin, but also the catechism. The language might be slighted, but the catechism—never! And since the job was really Bach's, he could not give up all responsibility merely by hiring another.

His primary job was to train the choirs, and at this he spent about an hour each morning. The rest of his time went largely into private instruction, both of the Thomaners and of the students who flocked in from every corner of Germany. He was never so in his glory as when a twenty-year-old sat at the organ bench with him, and he poured out the wisdom of his mind and fingers into an eager brain.

There was respite from his teaching and from the cantatas for at least ten weeks of the year, and he often took advantage of these holidays to go off on a pilgrimage. During Lent and Advent, the times of great preparation in the church year, the organ was silenced as a sign of humility. If there was singing at all, as in the hymns of the congregation, it was without the organ.

Of church festivals there never seemed an end. These often gave him a holiday from teaching, but caused extra work preparing a cantata. There was always music for the feasts of the Virgin, for Christmas, New Year, Epiphany, Good Friday, Easter, Ascension, St. John's Day, Michaelmas, and Reformation.

School holidays were frequent. At Easter, Michaelmas, and New Year, when the school terms began, there was a fortnight's vacation. In August, when the sun beat too fiercely upon the cobblestones and tiles, the boys had their afternoons free, and one could usually find them swimming, or lolling on the bank of a stream with a fishpole underarm, or on a long tramp through the woods. On quarter days and on saints' days, there was also no school. And whenever there was a funeral—nearly once a week—the morning was free.

In a city the size of Leipzig, you can well imagine how busy the choirboys would have been had they sung at every funeral and every wedding and every christening. Many of the burghers resented paying a fee, however, and did not especially care for the singing. Therefore they arranged their funerals and weddings in one of the village churches outside the walls.

There was no set fee for the use of the choir. Often

the whole group would sing, if the affair concerned a rich banker or a counselor or a lawyer. If it were for the stillborn child of a chimney sweep, on the other hand, perhaps only three or four would go, singing their hymns outside the house, in the church, and at the cemetery.

Any amount they were given as a tip was shared by the whole choir, and even the cantor and the rector had a small part. In fine weather such singing in the open air was splendid and healthful, but when the fog lay heavy upon the landscape, or snow covered the cobblestones, the boys were often sick with colds and coughs. Almost every day some of them were ill, for one cause or another.

Singing at a wedding or christening was enjoyable. Sometimes a host insisted on plying the youths with wine till they could no longer sing. If they had been at home under the care of their parents they might not have been so foolhardy, but at the school there were few to know and care. Their quarters were damp and poorly protected from the weather, and those who did not take special care of themselves were constantly ill.

During the weeks of the great fair which was held four times each year, the entire school would sing carols in the streets, giving special attention to the houses of the counselors and the well-to-do. For this they were showered with coins, and by the year's end, when the monies were divided, the sum gave each a handsome gift. The older boys and the soloists had the biggest share, as was right, and even the masters had something small for their trouble.

What worries Sebastian had at Leipzig, and they were many, were not about money. The basic salary for the cantorship was only a hundred thalers a year, but there were so many other sources of income that he usually earned seven hundred thalers.

In jest he sometimes remarked that seven hundred thalers would not go half so far in Leipzig as four hundred in Cöthen. Of course, he had but four children when he arrived in Leipzig, and another thirteen were later born to him and Lenchen. But no one could deny that potatoes and cabbages were twice as expensive in Leipzig as in the countryside.

With a large family, however, seven hundred thalers went a long way. Besides the cash, there was also the home and the cords of firewood. The money was not always certain, it is quite true. A good share of it came uncertainly from commissions—from the music Bach wrote on a nobleman's death or a duke's anniversary.

More came from fees at weddings and funerals, for his special compositions at the *Neukirche,* and from his share of choir money earned by the boys. Of this he had to pay out sixty to eighty thalers to pay a tutor in Latin and the catechism.

For all that, there was never any danger the family would go hungry. And Sebastian really did not care much about money, for often he would take a gifted young apprentice without fee as readily as one with.

On the other hand, he sometimes joked about the good weather being bad for funeral commissions, and the lack of taste of Leipzig couples who wanted no music at their weddings.

Bach's home was always stocked with nourishing foods. Likewise the furniture was adequate and up-to-date. Lenchen could afford one woman for washing and cleaning, and another for the cooking. With so large a house, and with thirteen children plus the four of the first wife, Maria Barbara, she managed well, though she had her hands full.

To pay for musical instruments there was always ready cash, and no one had such a fine collection, except perhaps the kaiser at Potsdam. Sebastian liked nothing better than a good clavier with pleasing tone and a precise action, and if one did not suit his taste after he had bought it he would relegate it to the children.

Six were still in the house when Bach died, as well as half a hundred other instruments. This is hardly to be expected of a man in financial straits. Bach's income was well above average, and during his Leipzig days he could never be called poor. If he did not live so well as the jeweler or cabinetmaker or surgeon, it was solely because he spent all his money on music.

11.

From Heaven Above

OF all the books in Sebastian's library, he loved best the works of Luther. In the column next to Luther's sermons, Bach wrote his own notes. What he wrote reflected his personality and his faith.

One sermon was of the story of Jacob—Jacob fleeing from the house of his father and taking shelter with his Uncle Laban—and of the night Jacob slept on a stone in the desert and dreamed of a golden stairway reaching to heaven, with hosts of angels on each step; Jacob vowed he would build a shrine, for it was there he had seen God.

When Sebastian first came to Leipzig with the text of his *St. John Passion* (before he was ever appointed cantor), he was as filled with religious vision as Jacob. He did not yet know he would one day be called there, and finish out his life under the roof of St. Thomas. But the impression of the organs, the skill of the organists, and the training of the choirs were like the vision of Jacob's golden staircase dotted with angels. Under his hands he could imagine them joining in one vast hallelujah to God.

When he was actually cantor, however, and had begun to write his cantatas, he saw how much sweat there had to be before he could achieve his vision.

He loved nothing so much as hard work. If hard work would accomplish the highest goal his imagination could set, then he would still have it.

At the heart of divine music Bach put the human voice. All by itself, he said, it is an oboe and a flute and a clavier and a violin and a cello. And if one takes a voice—a very ordinary voice—and trains and inspires that voice, it will produce a kind of magic that is finer than the finest of instruments. Sebastian had had that sort of voice as a boy, and he knew how much it could do for the praise and glory of God.

He was hampered, he knew, on several scores. For a year there had been no cantor. Before that, Kuhnau had been old and negligent. What boys were at the school were untrained, both in voice and on instruments, and he well knew that three or four year's hard work lay ahead before he could bring out the best from his boys.

What dampened his spirit most was discovering that many of the boys had been chosen without any gift at all for music. The best had moved on to the university, where they could sing with the opera.

From the first he set high standards. If he taught the Thomaner to sing well, and to sing only what was good, and if he taught the burghers what was best in sacred music, he could finally achieve what he dreamed. If he miscalculated, it was because the performers or the listeners were untrained. With time on his side, he could cure even that.

One block of musical talent lay untapped, and Sebastian dug for it as conscientiously as any miner in his native Thuringia. This was the group of students at the university. Of violinists and tenors and flutists there was a rich load, with the interest and experience that makes for real musicians.

Twenty years earlier George Telemann had been a student in Leipzig, and had gone straight from his studies to the organ of the *Neukirche,* under Kuhnau. With his own librettos he had written opera after opera, until the music, whether sacred or secular, had reached a high peak. Bach's goal was to implement the boys from St. Thomas with those from the university, and thus form a chorus and orchestra that would be matchless.

Winning the university would not be easy. Over the decades a tension had built up between the two schools. The council had canceled the endowments which Telemann had once used to pay his performers, and this did not make the solution easier. Still, if Bach could produce the kind of music that would catch fire in the hearts of his hearers, he would win support everywhere and the money would come afterward.

He did not win all the talent from the university but he did win some. For festivals he had on call twenty or thirty singers, at varying levels of skill. Counting seven players from the town band, he could make up an orchestra of eighteen—violin, viola, cello, double bass, oboe, bassoon, flute, trumpet, and drum. They were not all professionals, either singers or players, but with extra rehearsals he expected to bring them to perfection.

As soon as his family was well settled under the roof of the *Thomasschule,* Bach laid his plans. He would make a Christmas pageant more dramatic and skillful than the *St. John Passion.* There would be plenty of time to rehearse, for there were never any cantatas during Advent. He would have four wonderful weeks to make his musicians as lyrical as larks and as punctual as cuckoos. He would make the *Magnificat* the best Christmas gift Leipzig ever had.

Christmas was a three-day event, with services not only on the day itself but on the two that followed. To replace the regular service completely was not desirable, but Bach consulted long with the *Pfarrer* to bring his plans into line. In the end vespers became a service of music, provided as many of the texts as possible were scriptural.

Sebastian laid his plans early and there was time to write well. For five of the six services he would compose cantatas more flowery and elaborate than usual. But for Christmas day there would be something special. He had persuaded two young soloists from the opera at Dresden to give their voices to the church as a Christmas gift.

Christmas that year brought the sort of weather one finds only in story books. There was no fog or soot, just a clean, cold crisp in the air, and four or five inches of fresh snow. The row of fir trees at the Torgau Gate dropped low, with the hazy green of the needles half buried under white blankets.

For two days the sun shone brightly; not warm, but from a clear sky. The snow underfoot crunched at the weight of a boot, and the carriages skidded frequently on the cobblestones. From time to time there was a light flurry of powdery snow, like a frosting, in spite of the clear sky.

The children enthusiastically played snow games. After church that morning Friedy lay in the snow and flapped his arms in a half circle to show his younger brothers how one made a pattern of angel wings. Another time Lenchen would have been cross to see him treat his best clothes so, but because it was Christmas she smiled and said nothing.

In the shop windows were rows of fat geese and ducks, and lingenberries and sausages and cheeses that made mouths water merely to look. The bakers and the candy-makers had dressed their windows even more gaily than had the butchers and the grocers. One of them had a boy-size Hansel and Gretel house with a chocolate roof and peppermint chimneys, tiles of fudge and bricks of marzipan.

To sit around one's fireside at Christmas, surrounded

by the excitement of the children and the devotion of a loving wife, is in keeping with the spirit of the season. Bach appreciated it as much as anyone. But he had deeply entrusted his talents to God, and his home life was dwarfed by his religion.

Many worshippers from St. Nicholas were at first reluctant to give up their vespers on Christmas day, for the sake of principle, but they had heard so much about the pageant at St. Thomas' that they were curious.

For weeks the mothers had been mysteriously sewing costumes, and the boys had been whistling a tune or two, or some burgher had caught a magic strain wafting out into the square from the lighted windows of the church.

Dusk falls early in December and the sky was already gray when the worshipers scurried beneath the doorway of St. Thomas', with its huge spike on each corner and its odd little cupola over the roof.

A magic scent of forest spruce and fir hung lightly on the air, and garlands of greens draped from pillar to pillar. From the end of the pews jutted a row of candles, and the guttery light and the scent of tallow stirred the imagination.

In a back corner the young vicar had set up a crèche for the delight of the children. The figures of the shepherds and magi who knelt there were more German than Oriental, and the childish eyes that gazed on them oh-ed and ah-ed as if they had never seen such a miracle.

Because there were so many children in the church, the deacons had arranged for extra braziers of charcoal. The soft red glow of the embers and the trace of smoke put a spell into the air. In the organ balcony there was stirring, and as the last of the worshipers crowded in from the shadows by the organ a trio of trumpets sounded a compelling call to worship.

In a minute or two the entire orchestra had joined in —the violins and the violas, the flutes and the oboes. Their notes had a lively sparkle, like gems, polished clean and bright. More than one mother had to keep her youngster from humming in time, or from beating the rhythm with his feet.

When the voices of the choirboys swelled out it seemed as a heavenly host. If one could have seen clearly in the dim light of the candles, many an eye would have shown a tear. The church was deathly quiet. There was no sound but that of the musicians, and every ear was attuned to the music.

In the *Magnificat* were four episodes, each with its own music: the announcement by the angels, the birth of Christ, the visit of the shepherds, and the coming of the wise men. Of them all, as Lenchen later often told the story, the most effective was the announcement to the shepherds.

In the rear balcony the blend of instruments and voices and organ flowed smoothly along, and just as it reached the point of fullest appreciation, the tiny organ loft high in front of the chancel, where the centuries-old organ still stood, suddenly blossomed with candles. Simultaneously the birdlike voice of a boy soprano floated down and across the pews. His robe of white would have made him appear an angel even without the angelic voice.

He sang of the birth of Christ in the manger at Bethlehem, in the words every child had learned at his mother's knee:

From heaven above to earth I come
To bear good news to every home;
Glad tidings of great joy I bring,
Whereof I now will say and sing.

To you this night is born a child,
Of Mary, chosen virgin mild;
This little child of lowly birth,
Shall be the joy of all the earth.

These are the tokens ye shall mark,
The swaddling clothes and manger dark;
There ye shall find the infant laid
By whom the heavens and earth were made.

There was something thrilling in the tune and in the setting when that single voice wafted out across the rafters in a melody dear to every heart. The congregation knew that afterward, when the sermon was finished, it would take up the refrain itself. It would bring back their childhood, when they had first learned to know God in those words of the old hymn of Luther, written for his own children:

Ah! dearest Jesus, Holy Child,
Make Thee a bed, soft, undefiled,
Within my heart that it may be,
A quiet chamber kept for Thee.

Glory to God in highest heaven,
Who unto us His Son hath given!
While angels sing with pious mirth
A glad new year to all the earth.

The pageant which had been launched at so dazzling a pace never dimmed. The music continued to shift back and forth from the choir in the balcony to the one in the chancel, and sometimes to singers on the platform before the nave.

The town boys from St. Thomas who had no gift for singing filled in as shepherds, with the vicar in charge, and two others were dressed as Mary and Joseph.

Back and forth the music floated, telling of the prophets and the shepherds. The wise men came too, bringing their gold and frankincense and myrrh. And when all were gathered to adore the infant Jesus, "Joseph" and "Mary" rocked the child to sleep in the old custom nearly every family observed on Christmas Eve.

What made it especially sacred there in church was the grandeur of the music. The five soloists had now joined in a faint lullaby, prophesying that the rod of Jesse would bring forth a Son of the lineage of David.

One could spend many hours discussing the Christmas *Magnificat,* and the intriguing touches of artistry and devotion Bach brought to it. You could recall the mystery plays from which he borrowed the idea, and mention the less splendid attempts which Kuhnau had made before him in the *Thomaskirche.*

But it is simply impossible to describe the original performance of the Bach *Magnificat* without sounding overly sentimental. Though you can again experience the mystic pull of the music when you hear it, and though you can imagine the events of the pageant, no one who was not there that night will know how truly wonderful Bach's Christmas gift really was.

12.

Sunshine and Storm

BACH's greatest difficulty at Leipzig was the town council, which had become like a pack of crotchety old dogs squabbling for hours over meatless bones. The disease was catching, and it affected the faculty at St. Thomas until everybody was strained and nervous. The masters became constantly on the defensive, and none of them trusted his neighbor.

No one likes strain but Sebastian felt the disease would cure itself in time. There was much work for him to do at the school and in the churches so he buried himself in his music and steered clear of the council.

Besides doing the cantatas for the church and the odes for the university and the *Feststücke* for the court, he felt he could serve best by creating a love for the finest in music, and by training the gifted among his pupils in a technique that would endure. Among the Thomaner perhaps only a third would make real musicians. Whether or not they might one day serve the church with their music, Bach nevertheless felt an obligation to all, even those who would be listeners only.

His technique was so sparkling and unparalleled that a good word was said for him in every corner of Germany. His travels with Prince Leopold and his friendship with scores of musicians had made his name a byword among teachers of the clavier and organ, and whenever a lad reached the stage where he needed the greatest of tutors he was shipped off to Leipzig.

One of his most faithful students was Chris Altnikol, who later became his son-in-law. According to the usual pattern he first accepted Chris on a scholarship to St. Thomas', and when the boy had proved his willingness to work and his ability to play he invited him to live in the garret, where he could supervise him more closely.

Bach's mind was kept off the troubles of teaching and the squabbles of the counselors by his students. He was not sure his cantatas would outlive him, but he knew a young mind kindled with a fire for music and trained with a Bachian tenderness and thoroughness would be a lasting memorial.

Once his quarters were enlarged, he became more and more obsessed with his obligations toward his students. These were mostly pupils at the school, but now and then there were older ones past their teens. For the most part he preferred younger students, and would often make a spot for them at St. Thomas' even if he had to pay a few thalers from his own pocket.

When you think of the hours and hours he spent with each student, and make a mental list of the dozens he taught, you must admire his patience and energy. He won these young hearts to a point where they gave up everything to study under him. His stay at Leipzig was long enough for him to teach many teams of father and son. Often a father had such vivid memories of his teacher he insisted his son go nowhere else.

Such a team was the Krebs family. The younger Krebs had learned as much from his father as he was able, and had gone on to study under Bach. In German the name Bach, you know, means brook, and Krebs, crab. Once, at a wedding feast, Sebastian joked that the young man was the only Krebs in his Bach. That is to say Krebs was a fly in the ointment.

There were always four or five apprentices studying under Bach. The luckiest were those who could live in his home, and share his genius more fully. Kirnberger was one of the best of these, and the relationship was that of master and disciple.

Kirnberger was very proud of Sebastian, and would clench his fists in anger when a student called Bach by his nickname, "the old wig." Kirnberger eventually won an organ position in Berlin, and the musicians there were long amused by a story that shows how close he and Bach were:

A linen merchant from Leipzig arrived in Berlin on

business and came around for a visit with Kirnberger. The two Leipzigers had known each other as boys. Over the clavier in the sitting room Kirnberger had hung a portrait of his old master. Bach's picture served as a guardian eye, to remind him he should be faithful to only the best music and to inspire him when the composing went too slowly.

The merchant burst out laughing when he saw the place of honor was given to "only the old cantor from the *Thomasschule.* Why not get a picture of a duke or a prince?" he asked. Kirnberger was so angry he chased his visitor out, then ceremonially swept up the dust from the floor lest he bring dishonor to the name of Bach.

You might think Sebastian would have been sharp with those who wanted their music for purposes other than the church, or with those who were not Lutheran. But he was a great man and he loved music highly. One of his most gifted clavierists was Goldberg, who was of Jewish birth. Another was an Italian Catholic, Cavatini. Had he lived, Cavatini might have been the most famed of all, for he was unusually gifted.

When Bach and Cavatini were not talking religion, they were talking music. And had it not been for the swarm of Sebastian's children, Cavatini would doubtless have talked his master into a trip to Italy. Sebastian's fame might have been even brighter if he had left Germany, if only for a year, to visit France or England or Italy.

But if Bach did not go to the mountain, the mountain came to Bach. Hardly a week passed when there was no foreign visitor at the Bach table. In spite of the thirteen children she bore, Magdalena was a diplomatic and kindly hostess and a loving and competent mother.

The only foreign musician of importance who did not visit Bach was Handel. Handel was a native of Halle. While Sebastian was still at Cöthen, shortly after the trip to Hamburg, he heard Handel was in Halle and determined to visit him. Handel would doubtless have heard of Bach as a gifted performer, for they had friends in the same musical circles in Hamburg. When Sebastian reached Halle, much to his disappointment he learned Handel had left that morning by stagecoach.

When Handel came to Halle ten years later Sebastian was in bed with flu. It was all Lenchen could do to keep him in bed, he was so eager to meet Handel. Instead Bach dispatched a cordial note with his son Friedemann, asking Handel to give a performance or two in Leipzig. Unfortunately Handel thought it inconvenient and, it is suspected, rather provincial compared with the royal court of England.

In the Bach apartments at the *Thomasschule* there was always music in the air. By daylight you could hear one instrument after another, often to the background of the great organ in the church. Around the table or before the fireplace the talk was generally of music. Even when he was with his children on a picnic Bach could not hear the laughter of a lark without listening in terms of notes on a staff. His son Friedy said he could look at a row of clouds and form them into a melody.

His life simply overflowed with music, and one musician or another was always at his door. Even *Herr* Silbermann, one of the richest and most renowned builders of organs and pianos of the day, used to visit with Sebastian, not because he agreed with him but because the cantor might let something drop that would be of use to a builder.

Sebastian suggested that Silbermann temper his instruments so they could be used together with strings or woodwinds. In this the merchant was of the old fashioned school, and he was probably thinking more of his customers wishes than of the quality of the music.

Of one thing Bach did convince him, and that was a proper length for the keys. Patiently he would explain how one could play well only when the fingers were curved, not flat, and that it was far more convenient, when there were as many as four manuals on an organ, if the keys were not overly deep.

Bach's home was a house of music. What money he did not need for food or the education of his children he invested in music and instruments. The school itself was rather poor in its instruments, thanks to the niggardly attitude of the counselors. Bach was forever loaning a violin or a flute to a student who was hampered without a fine instrument.

Of claviers the school owned none, though there was one in the balcony of the church. But at Bach's there were ten. Conscientious Lenchen dusted and polished them as carefully as she fed her youngsters.

Of other instruments there was more than a roomful —violins, violas, cellos, flutes, lautenclaviere, a lute, a viola da gamba, a bass viol, a piccolo. Almost every wintry night Sebastian would have a *Musikabend* in his home. Often as not there were several students from the university and several Thomaner, and a few friends from the town band or the musician's union, with enough of the Bach children to make a band of their own.

The four children from the first marriage were entering their teens when they came to Leipzig, and all were gifted in music, whether with voice or instruments. Of course there were also all the youngsters who came along year by year to Sebastian and Lenchen, thirteen more in all. Of these only six outlived their childhood.

No one could have been a member of the Bach family, even by adoption, and been unaware of the musical genius who headed it. But what one noted most keenly was the sense of unity and devotion which was as solid a part of Sebastian as his music. It was a mixture of kindness and responsibility and learning and fatherliness few families have, the kind of tenderness that would make a busy father give music lessons to each of his children.

We should not forget the *Frau* Cantor, however. Magdalena was as steeped in the love of her children and her husband as a mother can be, and her stepchildren mutually adored her. She nursed them when they were ill, and comforted them when they were discouraged. Few women have had such a compliment as Lenchen, the morning she sat at the clavier and found there a poem written by her husband:

> If you are near, I go in joy,
> To death and rest reposing,
> How pleasant death, if with thy hand,
> My faithful eyes were closing.

13.

Surveying the Battlefield

MUCH to the amazement of Bach's friends, the dour Leipzigers mistook Sebastian's genius for pride. The three rectors of the *Thomasschule* —the two Ernesti's and Gesner—typified the attitude of the whole town. None of the three was an out-and-out enemy, yet each, especially the two Ernesti's, resented a man in their midst who was obviously their superior.

The first of the Ernesti's was Johann Heinrich, who was already a white-haired old goat when Sebastian and Lenchen first unloaded their furniture into the wing of the *Thomasschule*. Ernesti had little time for the classroom, except for the lectures he had been reciting year after year, and spent what energy he had at the university. Many of the later troubles at St. Thomas' stemmed from his carelessness and laxness, though he was unaware of what was happening.

At the time of Bach's arrival the job of cantor was growing as tangled as a ball of yarn. For centuries the cantor had been director of music for the university, besides chief musician of the churches. The university had never been happy about the arrangement; in its growing rivalry with St. Thomas' it made the university a second fiddle.

In the year that intervened between the death of Kuhnau and the arrival of Bach, a young musician who had taken Telemann's place as leader of the musician's union had begun to call himself director of music for the university. The title in itself was not so important as the prestige and the fees. When Bach arrived he was more than a little irked at the situation.

In his letters Bach signed himself not only as *cantor* but as *director musices*. When he added the honorary titles of *Hofmusicus* to the court of Weissenfels and Cöthen, it was indeed an impressive signature. For a time he ignored his rival, but the university was constantly depriving him of one or another fee that had traditionally belonged to the cantor.

The twenty-seven-year-old who opposed him was in effect a tool of the university. He had only mediocre gifts in music, but this was hardly a deterrent to one so hardheaded at Johann Gottlieb Görner. Even with the good will of the university, however, Görner could not win the respect of the students. When it was they who chose, when it was their cash that went to pay for a birthday ode or for organ lessons, it was to Bach they turned.

The relationship was complicated. As cantor, Bach had sole responsibility for the music in the four churches. But at St. Nicholas the organist who worked under him was none other than Görner. Previously, at the *Neukirche,* or university church, there had not been regular Sunday services.

When these were begun, a few years before Bach arrived, Kuhnau sensed the university might try to pry them away from the old jurisdiction, and he offered to furnish a choir and an organist without cost.

At the moment of Kuhnau's death, Görner grabbed the reins. His duties at St. Nicholas prevented him from directing or playing at the *Neukirche;* nonetheless he usurped the title and the fees. No one knew what to say when Bach complained, neither the town council nor the university. For years the dispute went unsolved.

Since the founding of the university there had been eight traditional services annually. These celebrated the four major festivals of the church year—Christmas, Easter, Pentecost, and Reformation—and the four quarter days marking the end of the term. The quarter days were when degrees were awarded, and they coincided with the fair. For graduation the director of music was to compose an ode; his fee would be rich enough to outfit him in a suit of clothes.

Sebastian had not been in Leipzig more than two months when he directed his first ode at the university. He was so enthusiastic he invested his fee in a Christmas gift for his oldest son: a year's tuition at the university, six years before Friedemann would even graduate from the gymnasium.

At first the townfolk sided almost completely with Sebastian, in spite of the intrigue of Görner and the officials. He was not only capable but he had age and tradition on his side. But this did not stop Görner from using the title of *director musices.* In fact, he once wrote it was he who, at the university, had brought to perfection what little skill the students had begun to learn when they started under Bach.

Görner's little talent made him hardly safe to accompany a cantata, so unsure were his fingers. Oddly, in their personal relations Bach was most cordial.

Only once did Sebastian completely lose his temper with him. He had mangled a cantata, not only playing the wrong notes but coming in far too early. In a cry of despair Sebastian flung his wig at the young man and said it would have been far better if he had been a shoemaker.

A professor of jurisprudence at the university was much taken with the new cantor and drew up for him a legal document to force the university to name him director of music. Actually Bach had been filling the post for two years, performing all its duties. What irked him was that the fees were going to Görner.

Finally the case came before the high court at Dresden, where the electoral prince had his seat. The judge ordered the title and fees assigned to Bach. If this did not put a final stop to the bickering, it was at least a moral victory. Unfortunately those who agreed with Görner were hard losers, and they spread gossip about the cantor and made his life miserable.

If Sebastian had known how his troubles would blossom in the next years he might have withdrawn the lawsuit. Görner had an uncle on both the council and the consistory, and even though beaten he could still bite.

One of the minor irritants was the choosing of hymns for services. To pick the chorales and to see that they harmonized with the gospel and the epistle had always been the work of the cantor. He could coordinate this and blend it with the text of the cantata. Each week he would make his selections and hand them to the chief pastor for final approval.

The young vicar who spent long afternoons with Görner was first to dispute the old custom. He was so eloquent he convinced the other clergymen. There ought to be some musical supervision, he admitted, lest there creep into the church a melody which had been sung in the tavern the night before.

On the other hand the sermon was so important that a dedicated preacher must have the right to choose a hymn to match his theme. Also most folk thought the list of hymns was sacred, and if you did not sing the same hymns on *Quasimodo Geniti* as you had sung the year before, the world might crash.

Under normal circumstances Sebastian probably would have agreed, for the suggestion had its merits. But at the time he felt everyone was trying to undermine his position. He objected so long, especially when he learned Görner had a voice in the argument, that the superintendent himself had to take a hand.

Old Salamo Deyling was one of the noblest superintendents the Leipzig church had seen in many a generation. He was ten years older than Sebastian and a friend to whom he could always turn. As spiritual leader of the diocese he was responsible for a hundred parishes, but he was never too busy to sit for a few minutes and listen to the Thomaner working through their Sunday cantata, or to take a minute or two to buy a stick of peppermint for young Emanuel or Christian.

Often he helped iron out the text of a cantata which sounded rough, and Sebastian felt especially close because he knew he and Salamo were in the same boat in their dislike for the town council.

When Ernesti died, it took half a year to call a successor. In this interval Sebastian took over countless new responsibilities at the school, which included making sure the boys were in bed at night and supervising their meals. When a new rector was appointed he proved to be an old friend from his Weimar days, Matthias Gesner.

In the school, at least, Sebastian's lot took a happy turn. Gesner put order into a situation that for years had been running wild. For the cantor there were new instruments and music, thanks to Gesner's influence over the council.

However capable, the new rector was not completely happy at St. Thomas'. In spite of his learning he was forbidden to teach at the university, as his predecessors had always done. The council wanted not a scholar but a schoolmaster, who would rap the boys across the knuckles and leave real teaching to someone else.

Gesner was faithful to his oath of office in whatever he did, even in his smallest promise. One could almost see his personality in the twinkle of his eye. With the council he never felt he had a free hand, and four years later, when the University of Göttingen offered a professorship, he leaped at the opportunity to leave.

Sebastian knew that in many of his disputes he overstepped the limits of Christ-like charity. A house guest once heard him at his prayers. He did not speak with pride, for he thought no one was there. "As you have multiplied in me the talent for music, O Lord," he prayed, "multiply also my understanding of others, that I be not hasty or unkind."

Perhaps he may have been thinking of his relations with the council. It is true they were more sinning than sinned against, but it was *they* who were the musically unlearned merchants and bankers and farmers and *he* who had the vision and breadth of genius—who should have had three times as much patience as they.

A typical incident occurred when he was rehearsing the *St. John Passion.* This was to be its third presentation, and though there were new boys for the singing there would be only a few changes in the text. Sebastian had started his rehearsal early but, much to his chagrin, one of the counselors, a retired farmer, came running into the church and ordered him to stop.

Any cantor would rightfully have been angry, but the council then rebuked Bach publicly because he had not first submitted the text for approval. That the same *Passion* had already been produced twice and that they had not desired to approve it previously shows they were looking for the smallest fault that they might demonstrate their authority.

Sebastian simply reported to the superintendent what had happened, and left the matter to Deyling. As it turned out, the consistory of the church sided with Bach against the council. But Good Friday came and went, and Easter, and there was no *Passion* at all. If he could not do it his way Sebastian would not do it.

On several occasions Bach was reprimanded because the council felt he was not fulfilling his duties. The charge rings untrue, for few spent so many hours at work as Sebastian. What was meant was that he did not direct his efforts in the way the council wished.

Bach did agree not to leave town without asking the permission of the *bürgermeister*. To one who rose at five in the morning and loved a jaunt in the country, sometimes by horse or stage, this was a serious bar to freedom.

If he had no classes, if his work was in order, he simply left. The council was fond of its authority and loved to summon at will the scores of people whom it employed. To find *Herr* Bach so independent was a rankling blow at its prestige.

Kuhnau had always treated the council with the same respect he would have shown a reigning king. When he put a request before them, he had carefully addressed them as "your Excellencies and right Nobles" and signed himself as "your most dutiful, respectful and obedient servant, the Cantor of the *Thomasschule*."

Sebastian was more businesslike, and though he was not disrespectful he did not fawn before them as if they were emperors. What irked him most was that they were constantly summoning him to appear before them. When it was *he* who requested a hearing before *them* to explain a plea in detail, they would order him to make his request in writing.

It had long been tradition for a new boy to come first to the cantor. If he met the musical standards, if his voice was good, the cantor would recommend he be accepted. After all, the purpose of the scholarships was to provide music for the church. If the money went to boys who were not musical, there was no point in giving them.

The school year began at Easter, and when the new boys were appointed one year Bach was horrified to learn he had interviewed none of them. The council had simply taken it into its own hands, in spite of the wishes of the cantor and the rector and even the inspector.

The choir was ruined for two years. When Bach wrote his annual report, he politely explained why. In his evaluation he stated simply that of fifty-four foundationers, twenty were partially trained, seventeen were untrained, and seventeen more were untrainable. The counselors thought him a pompous old braggart.

Then Bach was elected to direct one of the musical groups at the university. The timing could not have been better, for it gave him a chance to use some of the voices to fill the gaps among the Thomaner. Without them, and with the scholarships filled, the choirs would have had a sorry outlook.

The town fathers showed their displeasure at his new

interest in the university. Half a century before a music lover had left endowments to provide choirs for the churches. The fees that came to the singers were small, but to a poor student they were important. Since there was occasionally a chance to sing in the theater at Leipzig or Dresden, the endowments were often the difference which won the better singers for Bach.

When Sebastian took over the musical union, however, the council immediately cut off the funds. They said he could now use "*his* personality" rather than "*their* money," if he wanted singers. In the weeks before, he had composed and conducted the *St. Matthew Passion*, and later three magnificent cantatas to commemorate the two-hundredth anniversary of the Augsburg Confession.

When he had just done so much for the town, it seems the height of ingratitude for them to cut him off without a pfennig. When he turned against them, the fault was not one-sided. From that day forward, Sebastian lived for his music and his family and his students. He no longer concerned himself about the council.

14.

The Stops of the Organ

WITH a violin under his chin or a keyboard beneath his fingers, Bach lived in a world all his own, a world of mysticism and imagination. It was a rainbow world few others could penetrate.

This could have made him an absent-minded professor, but his daily contact with his family and apprentices and the Thomaner boys kept his feet on solid ground. Though a genius, his point of view was as practical as the butcher's or the grocer's, except that he saw it in terms of music rather than of roasts and cabbages.

A good illustration of practical music is the story of

the six chief parts of the Catechism. Luther, of course, had written the Small Catechism especially for the country folk in his native Thuringia. In one of his pastoral visitations he had learned that many who called themselves the children of God, even clergymen, did not even know the Ten Commandments, or the Creed, or the Lord's Prayer.

He and Melanchthon made the catechism a handbook for teaching, so that one who could not read at all or was blessed with only small learning could carry about in his memory at least the skeleton of God's plan of salvation. Most German youngsters by this time had to memorize the twelve or fourteen pages of the catechism, with all its passages from scripture.

Bach worried when he saw his children studying Luther's catechism and saw they were being taught mechanically. They learned the words but they did not come any closer in their hearts to God. For Bach's Friedy and Dorothea there were few worries. He knew family devotions and parental love would keep the children close to their Lord. What worried him more was the host of children who had no such example at home, though they came regularly to confirmation classes.

One pleasant day in May, Bach and the superintendent were jogging along the banks of the Pleisse. In a poetic way, old Salamo Deyling was as imaginative as Bach. "Why not teach the catechism with music?" he suggested.

After all, if Bach could entertain children at the clavier and keep them in peals of laughter, if he could musically describe a dancing bear at the circus or a drunken soldier in the barracks, why couldn't he do it with the Ten Commandments?

Here was quite a challenge. Sebastian knew that to write descriptive music about an animal is easy. To write about God is difficult. But with both Bach and Deyling rolling the plan around and around in their heads, it was not long before they worked out a plan. Deyling would write a short description about each of the six chief parts of the catechism, and Bach would write the music.

Most Leipzig mothers would have considered it a radical way to teach a child about God. But the cantor and the superintendent were too cagey to let anyone know in advance. Instead they simply brought the children into church in the usual way. Deyling began with a hundred words or two about each of the chief parts. Then Sebastian took over for five minutes or so on the organ.

As you know, the six parts are the Ten Commandments, the Creed, the Lord's Prayer, Baptism, Confession and Forgiveness, and the Lord's Supper. To paint a musical picture of these, Sebastian picked six simple hymns. He hoped the children would remember the words.

To keep the music fresh he did something he had never done before. He played the melody with both feet, an octave apart. Together with the words of the saintly old superintendent, and the turns and fancies of the music, the catechism sprang into life. One hymn followed another.

In "These Are the Holy Ten Commands" one could

almost hear Jehovah's voice as it boomed forth from Mount Sinai, giving the law to his people. In "We All Believe in One True God" there was a regular theme in three registrations, to represent Father, Son, and Holy Ghost. To present an idea so complex as the Creed was not simple, but Sebastian did this by depicting the grandeur of creation, the loving tenderness of salvation, and the pleasing lilt in our life when God works within us.

In "Our Father, Thou in Heaven Above" there was the trust and steadiness and inspiration that come from prayer, especially the Lord's Prayer. In "Christ Our Lord to Jordan Came," which tells of Jesus' baptism by John, you hear the ripple of the river and the rushing of the dove, and the voice of the Father saying "This is my beloved Son in whom I am well pleased."

In "From Depths of Woe I Cry to Thee" there was all the torture and anguish of sin, to depict the need for sorrow and repentance. More than one youngster was squirming in the pew, in proof of Bach's great skill at the organ. In "Jesus Christ, Our Blessed Lord" there was the sweet companionship of our Savior, and the reminder that in the Lord's Supper he can be a real part of us all.

Deyling talked for years of that session with the children. Many of them were still reminding him of it twenty years later. Had he bothered to consult their parents, or given the idea that the musical pictures were the responsibility of Sebastian, the town council would doubtless have raised a questioning eye, even though Deyling was chief pastor.

To Sebastian, however, it was all in the day's work.

Later he wrote the hymns into a practice book for Friedemann, but at the time he did not think the morning different from the usual Thomaner day.

Bach fell in love with the organ of the *Thomaskirche*. When he was late for dinner, Lenchen knew exactly where to send for him. It was indeed a good instrument, though not up to the level of those at Hamburg or Berlin or Vienna. The *Oberwerk* and the *Brustwerk* each had nine ranks of pipes, and the *Pedal,* five.

When Bach first came, the *Rückpositiv,* with its thirteen ranks, was connected to the manual. By separating it he could let the regular organist take the *continuo* and himself sit at the *Rückpositiv* for a descant. When needed, there was even the old organ over the chancel. In a pinch he could summon three instruments within a single church—a rare privilege.

The catechism hymns are a good example of a man so imbued with music that he can do nothing without giving it an artistic flavor—cannot even prosaically drink a cup of coffee or shave himself or shovel snow.

If he was visiting the home of friends and a child of the household was wakeful, he would sit at the clavier and produce a soothing lullaby. If he shared a drink with his cousin at Torgau, he would make a little fugue about the gurgling of the bottle.

If a nightingale was singing off in the firs, to himself he would hum the counterpoint. The fish at the market were not exempt from his playfulness, and one of his students who saw him sit at the clavier at a *Musikabend* and characterize the fishmongers said it was "so real one could smell the herring."

Of music more lasting there was never an end. One commission followed another, for an ode or a cantata or a fantasy or a motet. If it were not for a birthday or a coronation, it was for an anniversary or a funeral. At first the commissions came largely from the courts where his name was known, at Cöthen and Weissenfels. But as the students from the university scattered to the four winds, requests arrived from all Germany.

Sebastian loved his regular trips to Cöthen because they were an escape from the drudgery of the school and a chance to return to the circle of royalty. Since the petitions usually came in writing, and since the expenses were always paid, the counselors could not well refuse the request of a prince, though to them Sebastian was not a court *Kapellmeister* but an obstinate cantor.

Prince Leopold's first wife had died, and the second was as fond of music as the prince. On birthdays and anniversaries Sebastian and Lenchen were nearly always with their old friends at Cöthen, and they always took a musical offering.

When the prince made a grant to the council on one occasion, a choir of Thomaner traveled with Sebastian and performed a cantata. In this way Bach wrote many cantatas for Leopold: "His Highness Leopold," "Crown with Grace," and "Wave High Aloft" were the best.

In summer and autumn, when the courts were out of doors, Bach sometimes traveled from one to another as a kind of master entertainer. Of his formal compositions, dozens were of a scholastic nature. Nothing could happen at the university—the installation of a professor, the death of a dean, the anniversary of a founder, an award of honor, a birthday—without making it a musical event.

When Professor Kortte celebrated his anniversary, Bach wrote a musical drama he called "Unity in Discord." The two were such fine friends, often sharing one another's hospitality, that the wishes for health and happiness seemed as fresh and real as the words of children. His little musical jokes and the humor of the tunes were like the banter of bosom pals.

For comparison you might one day look up the score of "Happy Aeolus," which was written for the birthday of another professor, August Müller. The scheme is somewhat more formal, probably because Müller was the pedagogue sort, with never a hair out of place or a speck of lint on his waistcoat. The score requires a chorus of a dozen or more, and half again that many players, including trumpeters and drummers. The theme itself is exalted, as one would expect for a man of Müller's standing. It is the story of Aeolus, the god of the winds. One does not need gifted insight to hear the soft breezes of the South arguing with the gales from the North. In the end all works out happily, just like the scholarly dispute Müller had been having with certain scholars at northern universities.

The intriguing canons and skits Sebastian wrote for the delight of his friends he considered so trivial he often would not let anyone copy them down. With the notes of the keyboard running A through H, he often toyed with musical anagrams. Bach sometimes used his own name for a musical theme, flexing the rhythm and varying sequence to see what tunes he could improvise.

At the time of the fairs the city overflowed with musicians. Apart from fair time, the meetings of the musical clubs at an inn or coffee house were the highlights of the week. Sebastian liked them as a change of scene from his long hours at the organ, or the household of crying infants, or a council of complaining crones.

You can best catch the spirit of those evenings in their music. Lenchen's favorite was the *Coffee Cantata.* To understand it you must remember that coffee then was still a rare drink, for it was just being introduced from Turkey and Arabia. Lenchen first called it "the devil's drink," though in a few years she was drinking it by the potful.

One of the members of the musical society was Picander. He was more a poet than a musician, though in a pinch he could manage on the violin. To honor the opening of a new coffee house in Leipzig, the society voted to meet there. Picander wrote a clever poem, and Sebastian composed the music; this was the *Coffee Cantata.* The words give a good notion of what the townfolk thought of coffee.

The story tells of a royal order originating at Dresden that forbade all coffee drinking except by the king. Apparently the Leipzigers were already fond of their new drink, so fond in fact that the father in the story threatens he will never give his daughter's hand in marriage unless she promises never to touch coffee again.

As suitors wait upon her, she makes a vow to each. Unless he agrees to keep her pantry stocked with coffee, she will not even consider him. In the final scene everyone has a cup in hand, the princess has made her choice and the lovers are happily married, and coffee rules again as king.

This was a story so lighthearted and frivolous that it took the town by storm, with a musical trio everyone whistled for weeks. That first night Picander and Bach were carried home in triumph on the shoulders of their comrades. The *Coffee Cantata* is a good example of Bach's ability with the frivolous.

Those who knew Sebastian only in his last years sometimes thought of him as just a saintly old musician who could play the organ like an angel and write cantatas like an archangel. Yet he was never so saintly that he did not have time for fun.

Even in his younger years there was a stability and depth about him that many do not reach until the age of fifty. Of all his church music none is quite so moving as that which deals with death. In the calendar of the church the specter of death was never far absent, for it was the dominant theme of Lent, of the last Sundays in Trinity, and of All Saints' Day.

To Sebastian the shadow of death was more than a shadow. As a young boy he had lost both parents. He had grown up only a few years after the horrors of the religious wars that lasted for thirty years and killed off more than a fourth of the German people. In his own family, hardly a year passed that he did not lay one of his beloved children into the earth—ten little bodies, all told.

As a young organist he had expressed his deepest thoughts when he wrote an ode for All Saints' Day, to commemorate those who sleep in the Lord:

O child of man, you die not death,
Though blood and bone themselves lack breath,
You know that your Redeemer lives,
Who wakes you and salvation gives.

Lord Jesus Christ, Thy word is sure,
But make my faith in Thee secure,
Thine is the kingdom, Thine the pow'r,
And Thine the glory evermore.

Up, up, my heart! the day of God
Cancels out the night of fear,
Christ who slept beneath the sod
Long is risen from his bier.
No more can I hopeless be,
Jesus saved the world, and me.

Sebastian was not many years at Leipzig before he was commissioned to write the greatest of his dirges, the *Trauerode* for Queen Christiana. To know the place she held in the hearts of her people, one must know something about her background.

Christiana and Frederick Augustus were married in 1693, when Sebastian was a mere lad. As prince of Saxony, Frederick was not in line for the throne. In neighboring Poland, however, he was the crown prince. At the time of the marriage there was much gossip about the match, for Poland was strongly Roman Catholic and Saxony was strongly Lutheran.

Four years later Frederick was crowned king of Poland. To accept the Polish throne he had to renounce his Lutheran faith. Christiana had pleaded week after week with her husband. Not even a kingship, she said, was worth so high a price. But Frederick had few religious convictions. Whether a churchman wore a Roman cassock or a Lutheran frock was of little consequence, he argued.

Christiana refused to set foot inside Poland. With her son Augustus she took up quarters in a place symbolic of the Lutheran faith—Wittenberg. At sunset she often walked along the Black Cloister, where Luther had lived and worked.

The Saxons were never sure that King Frederick might not combine the thrones of Saxony and Poland and bring them under the sway of the Catholic faith. Four generations earlier Poland too had been a Lutheran stronghold, until the Jesuits of the Counter-Reformation drove out those who would not give allegiance to Rome. That, and the atrocities of the Poles during the Thirty Years' War, made the Saxons extremely wary. From personal experience, the grandfathers among them still spoke out in fear of the Poles.

As loyal subjects, in spite of the difference in faith, the Saxons celebrated the coronation of their king with solemn *Te deums.* They followed it with "A Mighty Fortress Is Our God"—cautiously lest they betray a shred of their Lutheranism.

From the time of the coronation there came incident after incident to annoy the Saxons. Though the king was not free to remarry, no one restrained him from living openly with Countess Königsmark. In spite of this he was honored by Rome with the title "defender of the faith." When his son came of age, King Frederick encouraged him with grants of money to desert his mother and come to Poland. The Saxons were even more perturbed when young Augustus became a Catholic.

Under these circumstances Queen Christiana lived a quiet and devout life in Wittenberg. Her stately figure, her motherly charm, and her saintly piety were an inspiration. In all the classrooms the little girls looked up to the queen as a heroine.

She did not have money to maintain a band of musicians, but each summer the manor where she lived was a mecca for roving players, who knew her fondness for music. Sebastian himself had stayed at her home, as had others, and respected her like a blessed grandmother.

Before the death of the queen, which greatly saddened everyone, there had been a vicious stabbing in one of the Saxon towns. The victim was a Lutheran pastor, and the murderer a Catholic layman. That the attacker was not altogether sane, the crowd did not realize. All they knew was that he was a Catholic, and he had stabbed a Lutheran pastor. The word spread quickly, and though the militia kept things under control all of Saxony was in a state of tension.

Under these circumstances the queen became a symbol of faith, resisting the call of money and of family at any cost. Her death brought universal mourning. All the towns and villages remembered her with poetry and song, with wreaths and memorials.

Bach was no little surprised when a friend of the royal family arrived one morning and delivered a commission for him to do a memorial dirge. It came to him not only because he was the best musician in the area, but because of his position with the university. At once he began to write and rehearse.

Görner made loud objections. He insisted that he, not

Sebastian, was the director of music, and all commissions must be cleared through him. True to form, the university backed Görner. But the royal agent plugged for Bach.

Trying a new tack, Görner said he must at least be allowed to share in the fee, and since Bach was composing Görner should conduct. Then the agent threatened to report the scandal to Dresden and to cancel the commission, which would be an insult to the whole town. Finally the agent offered a fee to Görner, though he had no part in the ode, as a consolation.

The university still tried to show its authority. Early one morning it sent the dean to get Bach's signature on a letter stating he would not again accept a commission to write any music to be performed at the university unless he first obtained the university's permission. The dean waited for an hour but Sebastian refused even to discuss the proposal.

Fortunately Bach did not let all this unpleasantness spoil his music. With the choir of Thomaner and the band from the university, he made the *Trauerode* a memory that would long give honor to the queen. It was longer than his usual cantatas, and in two parts to make room for the funeral oration between the halves.

In the music one can sense the subtle tenderness of feeling running from aria to aria and from chorus to chorus, as if some of her own saintliness shone through. The notes of the flutes rang sharply in a high pitch, like the bells of a church saying a last prayer, and the gambas and lutes called plaintively to a queen whose example had been so loved.

15.

The Battle of the Prefects

IN less than ten years at the *Thomasschule,* Bach had served under three rectors—the older Ernesti, Gesner, and the younger Ernesti. The differences in their personalities were as distinct as day and night. The first Ernesti was scholarly and antiquated, too old to concern himself with the welfare of the school. Gesner, in a four-year tour of office, put the gymnasium back on its feet, though his plans were often hamstrung by the council.

Under Johann August Ernesti the school was to change its face completely. Ernesti was only twenty-five when he was appointed assistant rector, and no one thought he would ever become rector. But when Gesner faced such opposition from the council, and took the fine job offered him at the university, no other successor could readily be found and Ernesti was eventually appointed.

The younger Ernesti was not a man of broad culture or education, though for the boys in their teens he was regular and orderly enough to keep the school from falling apart. He was not much older than Friedemann and had, in fact, stood as godfather for two of the younger sons of Sebastian and Lenchen.

At the university he had absorbed the new theory of education that was sweeping Europe. It accented the practical sciences like chemistry and mathematics, and downgraded the old classics such as Latin and Greek. Much the same sort of thing is found in the writings of Rousseau, and of course these ideas were the rage of the courts of Louis XIV and Frederick the Great.

In any case Ernesti felt St. Thomas' devoted far too much energy to music. He did not argue with Bach openly, but if he found a lad of talent in the choir he would slyly ask the boy if he hoped to spend his life playing a fiddle in a beer hall. In admitting new students he gave no preference at all to boys with a background of music, though the school had been founded as a choir school.

With ideas so opposite, it is not hard to see that sooner or later Ernesti and Bach would erupt openly. The dispute burst into flame in 1736, over the actions of one of the choir prefects. Among the six or eight oldest boys there was a kind of hierarchy, based on age and ability. The two with the most seniority were the prefect and the second prefect. Since the cantor could not direct three choirs at once in three churches, the prefects did a large share of the work.

Täter Krause was head prefect that year, and because the boys had been growing more and more unruly in the last months the cantor ordered Krause to keep a firm hand. One day Täter took the choir to a wedding, with council permission. As the affair was progressing several of the youngest, disobeying orders, tapped a bottle of wine and were soon throwing flowers and glasses about the room in a pitched battle. When Krause tried to control them verbally and failed, he became so angry he pulled off his belt and drove them out with a lashing of leather.

The storm would have passed had not an innocent lad been punished with the guilty, and had not his counselor uncle determined to make an example of the prefect. He went to Ernesti and demanded Krause's dismissal. From all accounts Ernesti agreed the prefect had exceeded his authority, and he ordered him to be publicly flogged, and in front of the choirboys.

Sebastian felt the punishment far more severe than the crime, and tried to take the blame on his own shoulders. "It was I," he said, "who told Täter Krause to be strict." But Ernesti wanted no one interfering with his orders, and refused to discuss the question.

Krause, though he was about to enter the university, left in disgrace rather than accept the flogging. The rector was so angry he would not surrender Täter's clothes, or the money he had earned. Some months later the council voted he be properly paid off.

What hurt Sebastian was not merely the undermining of his authority as cantor, but the injustice to his friend and student. The rector's obvious goal was to assure control over both music and musicians, making Bach little more than a door mat. Ernesti and Bach were greatly angered in the dispute but did not yet lose their respect for each other.

The second prefect was a Krause too—Johann Krause—and now the rector appointed him temporary prefect. Because he was next in line, Bach objected only mildly. Yet Sebastian stated openly that in the way he carried on with the girls and made use of the dice at the Half Moon, Johann was a disreputable dog. True, he had certain musical gifts, but he was not morally fit to be a leader of the impressionable young sextaners and quintaners.

A few Sundays with Johann Krause proved what Bach feared. The new prefect smelled always of wine and was totally unreliable. Sebastian called him in and explained he was being demoted once more to second prefect until he could improve his reliability. In his place Samuel Kittler took over. Sebastian discussed the whole matter with Ernesti, and it seemed settled.

But Krause got to brooding and complained so violently to Ernesti he was sent once more to Sebastian. Bach was never one to mince words, and he gave Krause four or five good reasons why he was unfit to be prefect. But Bach made the mistake of telling the young hothead not to keep seeing the rector—that Bach ran the choir, not Ernesti. The words were hardly out of his mouth when Krause hotfooted it to the rector, and the fur began to fly in earnest.

Ernesti put Krause back as prefect, and if Krause had not been so insolent the affair might have ended. But he was constantly ribbing Bach, a man nearly three times his age, and Bach ordered him to leave. Ernesti insisted Krause stay, and added that if Krause was not directing the choir at the service on Sunday the cantor would have to answer personally.

Matins came early during the summer, about five-thirty, and Bach went around to the vestry at sunup and talked the matter over with the superintendent, Salamo Deyling. He brought Samuel Kittler along to make sure there would be at least one prefect, and was told by the pastor to do as well as he could. On Monday they would all sit down and try to talk out the problem to a quiet ending.

The service was about to begin when Sebastian and Kittler reached the choir loft where Krause sat in the chair of the prefect. Bach pointed to the door, and there was not much Krause could do but leave. Ernesti did not often attend church services nor even school devotions, but this was one morning he dared not miss.

At vespers, of course, Bach had to be at St. Nicholas'. Ernesti arrived there before Sebastian, and threatened the boys that if they sang for any prefect but Krause he would cancel their scholarships. He brought Krause with him and sat down in the balcony himself.

When Sebastian arrived he became furious. He took Krause by the nape of the neck and pushed him down the stairs. The choirboys hardly knew what to make of the angry scene, but they knew better than to sing for Kittler if they wanted to stay at school. The only way out was for Bach himself to conduct, which he did.

By this time the dispute had grown so white-hot that Bach and Ernesti each lost his head. In a cool after-light both are proved wrong. Before the day passed each wrote a complaint to the council, and during the week that followed letter piled on letter.

The next Sunday the situation was nearly as bad, for the boys refused to sing for either of the prefects. There was music only because Bach himself conducted, and because he also recruited a student from the university who had sung at St. Thomas' some years before.

It was a matter of principle on which neither contestant was willing to yield. If Bach were to yield control of the music and of those who provided it, he would make himself subservient to the rector. On the other hand, he did not approach the question with an open mind when he allowed the original small incident grow to the size of a mountain.

The town council did not know what to make of the furor. Their relations with Bach were already so strained they might well have thrown all his letters into the waste basket. On the other hand Ernesti had also been giving them trouble. Why not let them both suffer? Apparently they decided to let the two protagonists battle it out, for the council discussed it but never made any recommendations.

As the months dragged on and still there was no solution, Sebastian knew he must turn elsewhere if his life were not to be embittered and embattled. He wrote letters to his friends in Prussia and Hamburg, in hopes he might find a musical post there.

Long before the dispute with Ernesti he had been producing considerable music for the court. His greatest effort had been the Kyrie and the Gloria he wrote for Frederick in 1633, which he later enlarged into the *Mass in B Minor.*

The *Mass* showed Sebastian at his best. It contained those parts of the liturgy which are found in the ritual of both Catholics and Lutherans. Though he was a loyal Lutheran, Bach had in mind a kind of testimony that in their music Catholics and Lutherans were still brothers. With all its detail and length, and with a double text—in Latin and German—it could hardly have been presented in a Lutheran or Catholic church. Bach probably intended it for a university group or as an oratorio.

For the elector it was an unusual gift. From painters in his realms he had had many canvasses, from poets, many odes, and from musicians, many scores. The elector's musical advisers hardly knew what to make of the *Mass,* with its vastness and its complexity.

Bach had had dealings in the past with the royal court at Dresden, when he had presented his case for the restoration of his fees as cantor, after the niggardliness of the council. Thinking of the friends he had made there, he did not hesitate to request a royal favor for his past efforts. He wrote:

> To your majesty I present this token of the skill I have acquired as a musician, with the humble wish that it may please you, not because of its merit but because of Your gra-

ciousness and understanding. For some years I have directed the music of the two larger churches of Leipzig. Through no fault of my own I have been vexed by the withholding of my fees, which may be stopped altogether unless your Majesty were to show his favor and grant me a patent as a member of the Royal Cappelle. If such be granted, I shall stand even more deeply in your obligation. Herewith I dutifully offer to prove my diligence in writing music for the church, or for your orchestra, whenever you desire it, and to devote my talents loyally to Your service, as Your Majesty's obedient and humble servant,

JOHANN SEBASTIAN BACH

The wheels of court grind slowly, if "exceeding fine," and Sebastian waited three years to get his appointment. A year after he had written the Kyrie and the Gloria, King Augustus chanced to visit Leipzig. It was October, and the reds of the oaks and the yellows of the larches ringed the town with a wall of autumn fire.

The council and the university were both eager to entertain Augustus as royally as they could. The quarterly fair was a good start, with its pageants and merriment, but in the best traditions of Louis XIV, who had raised royalty to new heights, they also must have musical entertainment. They were agreed that no one could work up an excellent program so quickly as Bach, even if they did not like the man, and with little time to spare they all pleaded with Sebastian to write quickly.

Bach took the group of tunes he had used a decade earlier for the anniversary of Professor Müller and expanded it to new heights. He had to tailor a new text as well, and when he was finished no one knew he had repolished old brass.

The theme of the cantata was lighthearted and skipping: King Augustus was not only elector of Saxony but also king of Poland. With Queen Maria an Austrian princess, the royal pair spread its roots far and the words gave due credit to both lands. The framework was that of four rivers, the Vistula of Poland, the Elbe of Saxony, the Danube of Austria, and the Pleisse of Leipzig.

In the music you could hear them flowing their separate ways, but flowing harmoniously in a pleasing commentary on the delights of nature. All praised the king, in a lovely counterpoint of colors and tones, but in the end the tiny Pleisse outvoted the others and claimed first rights on the king.

The royal couple was delighted by the production and, since they already knew Bach's name, the new pleasures he brought them had no little influence in the *letter patent* which made him a royal musician.

Part of this story happened a year or two before the outburst between Ernesti and Bach, but it is really all tied together since the squabble lasted two years. That it did not seriously annoy the council may have been because of Bach's age. He was well into his fifties.

Never afterward was there any question of his fees, or his right to conduct the music and the choirs. He did, however, lose much of his old influence at the council and the school. The officials felt he had been drastically unfair to appeal his case to Dresden. From then on he was left alone, with just an occasional touch of hostility. With no further harassments, he was able to use his new freedom and energy for his music. This was an admirable outcome for the sorry story.

16.

The Master Musician

HOW a man who could write every kind of music the world knows, should yet fail to write an opera was a constant puzzle to Bach's friends. Some guessed he wanted to devote his talents solely to the music of the church, though this would not automatically eliminate opera. There is no reason he should not have done an opera on a religious theme—Moses and Jehovah on Mount Sinai, with the giving of the Ten Commandments, or the Garden of Eden, with the temptation of Adam and Eve.

Doubtless the real answer was the musical climate at Leipzig, with the traditional cantatas of Kuhnau still having a strong influence on the leaders of the church. Had Sebastian been at Hamburg, where opera was flourishing, he would probably have tried his hand at it. And he was never unsuccessful at anything musical.

Certainly he enjoyed listening to opera. Every year he made trips to Dresden, which had one of the four or five finest companies in Germany. Whatever his reason for being there, he never missed hearing at least one operatic performance. When he went to Berlin a few years later to visit his son Emanuel, he regretted he had "picked the wrong time of the year." The doors of the opera house were shut for the summer.

At Dresden he often stayed not at an inn, but with friends. The most hospitable of these, and a frequent visitor at the Bach home in Leipzig, was the director of the opera, *Herr* Hasse. Hasse had married Faustina Bordoni, an Italian singer who was also the star of his troupe. Their home was always open to Sebastian.

Hasse wrote a number of operas, and of them all Bach preferred *Cleofide*. He was especially invited for the premiere and was an honored guest of the director. If he had been as opposed to opera as some of the Leipzigers believed, he would never have gone.

On the same trip one of the musical societies in Dresden asked Bach to give a concert. They had heard of his skill, but they expected nothing quite so dramatic and colorful. Before Sebastian left, the poet laureate wrote an ode which called Bach's playing "sweeter than the lute of Orpheus"—a most graceful compliment.

Two years later his son Friedemann was installed as organist of St. Sophia's. Though Friedy was a skilled performer, many of those who voted for him were remembering the skill of his father on the same organ.

Sebastian liked having a son in Dresden. It gave him a good excuse to travel. With the many babies in the household, he felt guilty about leaving Lenchen behind with the chores. Yet he was such a tireless traveler nothing could have kept him nailed in one spot.

His appointment as composer to the Saxon Court was granted in the autumn of 1736. It was customary to give a concert of acceptance. As soon as Advent began (when the church cantatas at Leipzig were omitted), he had leisure to head for Dresden.

On the first of December he sat down once more at the wonderful organ, new in Bach's time and which *Herr* Silbermann had completely rebuilt, and played to an audience as colorful and appreciative as any in his life—ambassadors, dukes, poets, counts, musicians, and princes.

Here, at a royal party, he had made the acquaintance of Count von Keyserling, the Russian Ambassador, who was to be a lifelong friend. Keyserling could neither eat nor sleep without music, and rather than keep a secretary or a manservant at his beck and call he employed a young musician, Johann Goldberg. Neither traveled without the other, and they did not stay at an inn where there were no instruments.

From time to time Sebastian would give lessons to Goldberg, who was as eager and gifted a pupil as any he had. Goldberg was not interested so much in the organ, as were Bach's other students, but rather in the clavier and the clavichord. He confided to Sebastian that he was seeking an especially soothing music, because his master often suffered from melancholy and sleeplessness. The only cure was listening to the clavier.

Sebastian said he could think of no music to fill the bill, but it would be simple to write some, once he got home. With the count so good a friend, it would be not only a duty but a pleasure. A few weeks later Sebastian forwarded the new compositions, a set of thirty variations for the clavier. For weeks Bach had no reply, not even a thank-you note. He began to wonder if his scores had arrived.

Instead of a letter the postal courier arrived one morning with a parcel. The wax seal bore the coat of arms of the Count von Keyserling. With Lenchen and Liesgen impatient at his side, Bach carefully cut away the cords. Within he found a silver snuff box and, inside, a hundred pieces of gold. Here was half a year's salary, and everyone was in such high spirits that Sebastian hurried around to the butcher's and bought a goose, to celebrate.

To have such good friends as Keyserling and Goldberg took the sting from the pettiness of the council, though its members could never quite stop harassing him. After he had returned from Dresden with the title of composer to the Saxon Court, they summoned him haughtily to a meeting to complain that while he was gone the prefect had pitched a hymn far too low and no one could sing it. In the future would he please train the prefects more thoroughly?

About this same time Bach made a trip to Kassel. The

Hessians have always been a proud folk, and they insisted on inviting not only *Herr* Cantor but also the *Frau* Cantor. From the minute they arrived in a rented coach and four, Sebastian and Lenchen were treated like royalty. They were given a suite of rooms at the best hotel, and a servant to look after them.

Everything was brought out: fine foods, good wines, pleasant entertainment. Bach did his usual superb job at the organ and so pleased the townfolk that they asked him to stay. The Bachs were there only eight days, but they were presented with such luxury that, with the fee and the expenses, the cost for the city came to a hundred and sixty thalers, nearly Sebastian's yearly salary.

When you realize how much time Bach spent away from home, and count the stream of weekly visitors, you wonder when he found time to work. Like Luther, he used to fall back on the proverb *"Morgenstunde ist Gold im Munde"*—"morning hours are money in the bank." As he grew older, the work of rehearsing the choirs fell more and more to the prefects, but he still rose at four or five each morning. At night, too, when the babies were tucked under the covers, he liked to retire to his composing room and for half the night his scratching quill could be heard. Morning and night he drove himself as hard as his still-sturdy old frame would go.

Often he kept under his pen a score he had begun years before. For one reason or another he was not satisfied, and would continually work to improve his version even when he did not expect to use it again. It was under these conditions he kept at work on the massive *St. Matthew Passion.*

This *Passion* had been given first in 1729, in his first year at Leipzig. The choirs that year were mediocre, and with the taste of the townfolk still rather primitive in their understanding of music the *Passion* had not been a complete success.

All the same, Sebastian knew the *Passion* was one of the most moving things he had ever written, and he felt he must keep revising, revising, revising if he were one day to try it again.

He waited more than ten years for the opportunity, then he proved that the first failure was not the fault of the music. By this time he could draw from the skilled musicians of the university, and on a musical tradition which had expanded and grown. Now the *St. Matthew Passion* became a welcome and moving event of Holy Week.

The custom of setting the passion story to music is almost as old as Christianity. In the parishes of Germany the practice gained new life at the time of the Reformation. George Rhaw and Johann Walther, the church organists who worked closest with Luther, wrote such music.

Heinrich Schütz kept the tradition strong and flourishing right up to the time of Sebastian, and of course you can still find congregations in Germany where such a work is sung every Maundy Thursday and Good Friday.

There were certain conventions the people held sacred, and these Bach did not throw out the window. The chief singer was usually the evangelist, whether Matthew, Mark, Luke, or John. He was almost always a tenor.

Jesus was represented as a bass, and his arias were never so flowery and melodramatic as those of the apostles. The role of the crowd fell to the chorus, and it was used both to carry the line of the story and to provide a background.

Given the rules of the game, Sebastian played it far better than any who came before or after. Actually he wrote passions on all four of the evangelists, though the one on the Gospel of St. Matthew is doubtless the most moving. Perhaps it is because of Matthew's text, and the depth of Jewish faith and flavoring that one finds in Matthew. Somehow the country words of Matthew are richer and stronger than the polished city style of Mark and Luke.

To make the voice of Jesus stand out, Bach accompanied it only with strings, so that it had a kind of tremulous and mystic frame. And to focus attention on the words and not merely on the drama, Bach worked out the phrasing with the poet Picander to achieve the proper touch of a gifted writer.

He did not want the hearer merely to listen to Peter denying his Lord, without any application. He wanted to put it so strongly the hearer would ask himself whether *he* was being a Peter. He did not want the crowd before Pilate to shout "Crucify him! Crucify him!" without forcing the hearer to ask himself if he also would have joined in the shout.

To learn the contents of the Gospels and to discover the work of Jesus, can be done in hours of meditation over the *Passion According to St. Matthew*.

17.

The Spice of Life

THERE always has been a vast gulf between one who is deeply convinced of his faith and one who is merely sentimental. When you listen to the music of Bach, with all its ties to the scripture, you are convinced he was not one whose religion was a mere sentimental attachment or, on the other hand, that he was a dour-faced old Puritan who never cracked a grin.

Neither is true. His faith was deeply integrated into all he did. Unless you had known him well you hardly would have realized he was continually working with choirboys and making friends among the clergy. When his eyesight began to fail he might have become gloomy and melancholy, but despite his troubles he had a quick and hearty laugh.

Guests and relatives were always popping in with new stories and adventures. His cousin Elias from Schweinfurth visited at least once a year, and from time to time he would bring a sample of that nut-like wine of lightest amber that grows up and down the valley of the River Main. Sebastian praised it so highly he was sent a full cask one Christmas.

He was more than a little pleased when the deliveryman knocked at the door, for it would be a proper treat for all the guests who came visiting during the holidays. Unfortunately the bung had not been tight, and there was scarcely a gallon left. All the same he appreciated the thoughtfulness, even if he had to pay such charges for shipping and delivery and customs that it became the most expensive wine he ever served.

The Thüringerwald has always been the home of birds, and there was hardly a time in Bach's life when there were not birds about the house. The linnets and thrushes he liked best, and sometimes when he could not come by a tune for a cantata he would have Friedemann fetch one of the cages into the *componierstube*. In less than a quarter hour he would be writing away, remembering in his music the bird that inspired it.

That he was something of a man about town is clear from the number of musical societies to which he belonged. He presided over the one that met in Zimmermann's garden, behind the mill. He also belonged to one that Görner headed, out by the monastery. These met week after week, to chat and to perform, and through these societies he cultivated many friends from the university.

More than one young men eagerly "sat at his feet," for he was considered the musical lion of the town. Others who were not musicians also came to respect him—folk like Christian Henrici, the young poet who used the pen name "Picander."

During the quarterly fairs he was so busy with performances that poor Lenchen said he did not take time even to eat. For this reason he hesitated for a long time before he joined the greatest of all the musical societies, Mizler's.

As proof of his skill, he wrote a canon for the society on the Christmas hymn, "From Heaven Above to Earth I Come." The members had his portrait in oils hung at the clubroom, which was located above the coffee house on the *Catherstrasse*. Sebastian expected to dislike the time he spent sitting for the painting, but it was not quite so bad as he feared. His mind could still be active improvising and recalling tune after tune.

It was at the fairs that Sebastian was reminded of the folk tunes of his youth. He could not see the bags of wool or the sacks of toys or the heaps of cabbage without casting away his dignity and becoming boy-like again, footloose and carefree.

He was not above taking one of the folk tunes and dressing it in a fancy costume. More than one of his cantatas had its birth in the bagpipe wail of a shepherd, heard years before on the hillsides of Eisenach. He sometimes used a nursery rhyme to teach his apprentices how to make a canon, weaving one part against the other. One of these was the standard jingle of a lad who didn't care for his mother's cooking:

Turnips and cabbage
Are mighty poor pasturage;
If my mother'd cook roast
I'd stay home to roost.

To watch the lightning flash in his eyes when something curious skipped through his mind during a conversation was a delight. This side of his personality can be seen in the story of the presentation of the *Peasant Cantata*:

The town of Little Ischocher was getting a new squire, Heinrich von Dieskau. He was born and bred a countryman, and had come into money from his father. When he became *Gutsherr,* or lord of the manor, Heinrich wanted to make his workers happy. After all, these villagers would be cutting his barley and grooming his horses and trimming his orchards and baking his bread. Nothing was too good for them—in a rustic way.

The *Gutsherr* had been to court often enough to know the foibles of royalty. He knew it was fashionable to hold not even a hunt without music. All over the country he had heard talk about Johann Sebastian Bach of Leipzig. Sebastian, people said, could make music even about the reins of a harness. So nothing would do but for Dieskau to send for Bach.

Sebastian and Lenchen were pleased with the invitation. For one thing, it was generous, and for another, it was lighthearted. With his usual polish, Bach put a musical skit together and brought with him two or three students from the university to sing the leads. The rest of the musicians he would find locally.

Von Dieskau sent his carriage for the Bachs and welcomed them heartily. It took them a day or two to feel at home, but soon they were finding the buildings and grounds of the squire very pleasant. Lenchen did not worry about the youngsters at home, for they were in the care of a conscientious maid. Bach happily took over the rehearsals on the quadrangle of lawn surrounded by the manor and the outbuildings.

If you've never been to a country dance or eaten at a country inn, where a bit of chaff drifts into your soup and the smell of cattle is in your nose, it's difficult to fully appreciate the mood of the *Peasant Cantata.* On that summer day in 1742, however, with Bach's lively music in your ears, you would have been enthused enough to snatch up a bagpipe yourself, or throw your arms around a pretty girl and swing her heartily into the dance.

Villagers came from miles around. The country gentry came too; their different country clothes were as fancy as those from Dresden, but smelled a bit of stale lard and of tamarack smoke.

There were leather chairs for the gentlemen and their ladies, but the villagers lounged on the turf, gulping from a jug of stout or a flask of wine. Against the far wall, conveniently placed so the singers could come in quickly and unobtrusively from the barns, was a little platform for the performers.

The lyrics alone are so infectious you feel the mood of the music just to read them:

We've got a brand new country squire,
An honest one, to boot,
The beer he serves
Inflames the brain
And that's the honest truth.

Let "preach" object, as preachers do
The fiddler taps a louder shoe
And dirndls swirl at every note,
Come on, come on,
Let's dance, you goat.

The skit made considerable sport of *Gutsherr* von Dieskau. When it was not laughing at the squire, it turned its fun on the villagers. Dieskau did not yet have a son to carry on his name, and there on the stage one of the villagers addressed his wife in the tuneful lyric,

Come, honey, make honey,
And give him a son,

Come, honey, make money,
Or Dieskau is done.

What made everyone laugh until all were rolling in the grass was the rustic clowning of the players, as heavy-handed as if an elephant were to dance a ballet. There was a blacksmith pounding on cymbals, a snap-second off beat, and Sebastian laughed cheerfully at himself when the chorus complained—

You're absolutely right,
My rhyme's a ghastly fright.
But blast the luck—I'm stuck again,
It's out of ink, this stupid pen!

Everyone squirmed with anticipation when a look off to the side showed a squad of cooks preparing the banquet. From the spits the aroma of roasting oxen and geese drifted pleasingly over the courtyard ,and serving boys moved among the crowd with salted herring and beer which whet the appetites.

Bach stood off at the side where he could direct, and once he picked up a dented old hunting horn, playing a wee bit off key to mock the bass viol.

The story was of a new landowner who came to the village desiring to establish good terms with those who worked his lands. It was a clever piece of work, blending all the folk dances and rustic tunes and country life so rarely seen in the city.

On stage it ended precisely as it would moments later in reality—with a big feast—for on the stage the singers chorused that they were headed to the village inn, where they could dance and eat and sing:

> We're off to where the groaning bag,
> Makes *sad* our village inn;
> We're off to where the bagpipe's moan
> Makes *glad* our village inn!

In impish mood, the singers danced off the stage into the barns, with a swirling of aprons and skirling of music that brought thunderous applause from the crowd.

Time and time again they were called out to repeat the closing chorus, with its catchy bagpipe accompaniment. Finally the *Gutsherr* had to announce the food would be burned to a crisp, if they did not stop to eat. He was laughing so hard he could hardly be understood.

A Bach entrancing a crowd of country bumpkins and a Bach holding spellbound the courtiers of Dresden, illustrates the broad base of Sebastian's genius. At St.

Thomas' his acquaintances missed his lighter side, though of course those who knew him intimately could always count on the cantor for a humorous anecdote.

With his children he was always spirited. Three of the four children of his first marriage, to Maria Barbara, had grown and left the family roof by this time; Dorothea, who had not married, remained. Of Lenchen's children, from the second marriage, five were still alive and at home.

Sebastian always made time for his children. Perhaps, in the light of later events, he loved them too strongly, if that is possible. When they were unfaithful to his ideals, he would worry and fret until he lost all appetite. Friedemann was dearest to his heart, and Sebastian regularly traveled to Dresden to visit with him.

But in his last years Sebastian could not bring himself to speak of Friedy, who had moved on to a post as cantor at Halle. The trouble started with too much wine. Friedemann had never been as stable as his father. Even as a lad he had frequent fits of melancholia and moodiness. At Halle he passed off as his own a cantata his father had written, which subsequently won high praise from the critics.

The authorities, however, refused to deliver the prize when they learned of the deception. The incident might not have happened had it not been for wine. Friedemann certainly could compose excellent music of his own, and do it well, but as he grew older he became lazy and shiftless.

The second son, Bernhard, became organist at Mühlhausen. where Sebastian once played. The council still had such affection for the name Bach they were most eager to have Bernhard and raised their offer to keep him from going to Torgau instead. But Bernhard also got into serious difficulties, and twice Sebastian had to pay up the boy's bad debts.

In many ways Phillip Emanuel, the third son, was more like his father than were the others. He had studied law and philosophy at the university, but he loved music so much he could not fancy himself in the wig and robe of a judge. For years he played as court musician to Frederick the Great at Potsdam.

Sebastian's visit to Berlin and his performance before the king could hardly have happened but for Emanuel. The son was as gifted at a keyboard as his father, and there is little wonder the king chose him to be his personal accompanist. Frederick had a good ear for music and, though he played only a few instruments, his skill on the flute was professional enough to earn him a living had he not been king.

Emanuel was not the only student of Bach who belonged to the royal orchestra. Six or seven others who studied at St. Thomas' also played before the king, and he kept hearing so much about Sebastian that he was eager to meet him. From time to time Emanuel would write of the king's desire, but Sebastian was fully occupied with the royalty at Dresden and Cöthen and Weissenfels. Berlin was too far away.

His mind was changed not by the king, but by the birth of Emanuel's first son. At the moment things were rather quiet at Leipzig, for two of the younger children were recovering from measles, so Sebastian judged it a good time for a trip. Besides, in spite of his own brood of children, a grandchild was something new in his life.

He arrived at Berlin on a Sunday evening and went to the quarters of his son, who lived in an apartment in the palace. As a guest in the king's lodgings Sebastian of course had to register, and no sooner did the clerk learn his name than he went running to the king.

Frederick the Great was a man of regular habit. Every night of the week that he was at home he held a musical entertainment, lasting from seven to nine. The servant who came before him knew Frederick did not like to be interrupted, but he had his orders to report that Johann Sebastian Bach had just arrived. Frederick heard the news with delight, and sent the servant to fetch him. Then he announced, "Gentlemen, old Bach has arrived!"

Sebastian was tired from the journey and hardly prepared to make a command appearance. But obviously he had no choice. The king had said to come as he was, without changing his garments. He did, but he felt out of place in his threadbare serge when he found the court assembled in velvet and satin. The walls glittered with mirrors and statuary, and reflected in the highly polished parquetry of the floor he could see his image. And banks of candles and braziers made the chambers as bright as day.

The king, however, received him with every kindness. Frederick was carrying the silver flute he often played, and the evening concert had been just about to begin. But with the arrival of Sebastian, Frederick changed the usual routine.

He insisted his guest sit down and play—play whatever Bach wished. Sebastian had been hoping for this invitation. Ever since he entered the room he had been admiring the pianos.

He had heard much of them from Silbermann, who built seven of them especially for the king, incorporating a new action imported from Italy. They were sheer beauty to look at, with the rich red of the mahogany inlaid with tortoise shell and silver. With Bach at the keyboard, they became sheer beauty to hear.

Sebastian praised their tone so highly, and his playing was so appealing, that Frederick was soon leading a pilgrimage from room to room. Before the tour was concluded, Sebastian had played all seven of the pianos. It was an exciting evening for everyone but especially for Sebastian, for he had never seen and played such fine instruments in all his life.

The king said he had heard much of Bach's skill at composing, and that it was claimed he could "listen to the whistle of a schoolboy" and immediately work out a beautiful fugue. "Is this true?"

Sebastian suggested the report was surely exaggerated. But the seven students who had known him in Leipzig chorused against him. Intrigued, the king played a theme on his flute which he had written a few days earlier, and suggested that Bach make some variations on it.

Sebastian, with a mischievous look, went at once to the keyboard. His music filled the room, as clever and as moving as usual.

When he had finished, he apologized profusely because he had done "no better thar a three-part fugue," which he hoped had been "satisfactory." Then Emanuel suggested a theme more suitable for a fugue, and Bach sat down again and worked it out fully, in six different parts. Before the evening was over and they all had withdrawn, the king was saying over and over there was no musician in all Germany quite so skilled as "Old Bach."

The next day Sebastian gave a command concert on the organ at the Church of the Holy Ghost. That night he played again at Potsdam. He enjoyed the good food, the fine music, and the joyful banter, for he was young at heart, and when he got back to Leipzig, Lenchen hardly knew him.

Perfectionist that he was, he could not at once forget the visit. Something remained to be done. He had made a mental note of Frederick's theme. So now, as he sat at his desk with quill in hand, staring out over the ripples of the Pleisse, he wrote a proper fugue. He was careful to write it not only for the piano but also for the flute, knowing that the king and Emanuel would be playing it together.

When it was perfect, he copied it in his best hand on fine parchment and sent it off to the bookbinder, who covered it with fine calfskin and imprinted it with gold. Sebastian titled it "Musical Offering" and sent it off to Potsdam, along with a note of thanks for his happy reception. Frederick, though he did not send a box of crowns as a reward as had the Count von Keyserling, treasured it as the finest of his music.

18.

The Setting of the Sun

AS HE did with several other of his children, Sebastian wrote out a fine leather music book for his son Heinrich, complete with tunes, exercises, and scales. Written in a careful hand and with a costly binding, it was far too fine to carry from house to church and home again, so Heinrich often copied out his daily exercise on a separate sheet of paper.

Bach wanted to remind his children of their obligations to God, so throughout their work books he copied verses from hymns, or poems from his own imagination. He wrote this for Heinrich:

Fall asleep, you fickle mortal,
Close your eyes in blessed sleep.
World, I stay no longer here,
Want no part of life so drear,
That my soul may pass the portal
Fall asleep, you fickle mortal.

Bach had always lived so close to his Maker that death was nothing to fear. Ten of his children had gone to death before their father, and the *Kirchhof* bore many stones engraved with the name Bach.

In January of 1749 Sebastian's old age was brightened by the marriage of his daughter Liesgen. He was especially happy to give her hand in marriage to Christoph Altnikol, who had been his loyal and gifted apprentice and had lived in the top floor of the Bach home. As a wedding gift, he procured a position for his son-in-law as organist at Naumburg.

For years Sebastian's sight had been failing. By midyear he could hardly see to play, and by the end of 1749 the officials of the school began quietly to look for a successor. Liesgen and Christoph were so perturbed by his turn for the worse they volunteered to return to Leipzig to help care for him.

During Bach's last months no one was quite so faithful as his new son-in-law. To him Sebastian poured out the full feelings of his faith. To the very end he was cheerful; to the very end he dictated music and letters every day.

By the spring of 1750 Sebastian could no longer see enough even to line out a staff or fill in the clefs. He could scarcely distinguish light from dark. In March an English surgeon living in Berlin had come to Leipzig to take the waters. His fame was great and he was urged to do what he might for old Sebastian.

The operation was not successful and the old eyes that at least had been able to distinguish light from dark were now totally blind. Sebastian took his loss with Spartan fortitude, but the pain was increasingly great. Sometimes even heavy doses of belladonna and nightshade could not ease it. But, suffering or not, his mind was constantly alert. He was constantly rehearsing in his memory a piece of music he had written years before.

Chris Altnikol and young Müthel, another student, were kept busy writing down his music. Bach dictated page after page and his memory astounded them both. He seemed to recall every registration and every stop, though the music might have been written a decade or more in the past.

He worked chiefly on the choral preludes, "Jesus Christ, Our Blessed Savior" and "Come, Holy Ghost, Creator Blest," recalling all the old harmonizations and humming a bit to jog his memory when he was puzzled. What changes he made were worthwhile improvements.

Because of his pain, the family encouraged him to keep busy and so forget the suffering. He loved also to be read to from the books of his youth, especially the sermons of Tauler which he had often read at the table as family devotions, and the commentaries of Luther, which had been textbooks for his children.

Day after day he worked diligently at his music. His wife Lenchen confidently expected he might still recover. His mind was as healthy as ever, but anyone not in the family circle would have seen how his body grew daily more wasted. The month of June gave way to July and still he lingered. More and more his thoughts turned to ancient hymns, and of these he found most comfort in those that dealt with death.

One of the last arrangements he dictated was "Wenn wir in höchsten Nöten sind." The words still ring clear and sure:

When in the hour of utmost need,
We know not where to seek or plead,
When days and nights of anxious thought
No help or guidance yet have brought,

Then this our comfort be alone
That we may stand before Thy throne
And cry, O faithful God, to Thee,
For rescue from our misery.

The pain of the eyes and the swirling of the drugs seemed to quicken his mind until it darted like a swallow. Hardly had be begun the prelude, reeling off line after line so quickly that Altnikol could scarcely get it down, when he was ready to begin another.

The mood of the second was even closer to the mood of death. "At the top of the page," he said, "write 'Vor deinem Thron tret ich allhier.'"

Before Thy throne, my God I stand
All that I am is in Thine hand;
Smile on me with Thy smiling face,
And heal my wounds with balms of grace.

For a few hours before death finally came his eyes could see—though it was a mere break in the clouds, not the end of the storm. No one dared to pull back the draperies at his windows for those tired old eyes would never have dared the brightness of a July sun. It was as if he were a Moses, with one last glimpse of the promised land before Jehovah finally snatched him from the earth.

The funeral was as simple and as musical as the hundreds of funerals for which he had played in the days when he had led the choirboys through the streets of the town. It was as if the comfort of Christian music could blot out the great sadness of death. From St. Thomas' pulpit Superintendent Deyling comforted the congregation and family, and, with Altnikol at the organ, the choirboys sang one of Sebastian's cantatas in loving tribute to their old cantor.

The bells of the four churches pealed resoundingly as if to accompany him into the earth. Representing the school, Professor Kriegel spoke a simple eulogy, and the Society of Music offered a memorial ode for voice, violin, and flute. The mood of the morning was as simple and sincere as if Sebastian himself had been in charge, and in a sense he was, for no one there had not been his friend or student.

Johann Sebastian Bach left a heritage of faith and of music which few have equalled. Of all his skills, he was most at home when he sat at the console of an organ. This is not to belittle the oratorios or the passions, the cantatas or the concertos. He was skilled alike at clavier or violin. But it was when he sat at an organ that he lost all sense of time and space.

His fingers flew from key to key like a modern computing machine gone mad, and his feet were no less active. To watch him from behind was dizzying, but to listen from a pew below with closed eyes would lead to heavenly dreaming.

While praising his skill, some of his students made him sound like a mad genius out of touch with the world. A few folk did think of him so. He loved his walks through the countryside; he would find a village church where he was a stranger, take a seat at the organ, and then, in a crescendo of inspiration, he would set the town alight with admiration which lasted for weeks.

He was basically a simple cantor who taught his boys to sing the praises of God. But there are many other things for which the world will never forget him: his general knowledge of all music, his tempering of the clavier, his games and jokes, his heroic little doggerel, his underlying faith—all these are inseparable from the real Johann Sebastian.

He did not seek gold and silver, though the opportunities were many. He did not run away from fame, but at the same time he did not really seek it.

He could be stubborn, as when the pretentious oaf Ernesti crossed his path, but he would have given his last groschen to put a pair of gloves on the cold hands of a child. He never traveled beyond the borders of Germany, though his musical scores were carried to the farthest corners of Europe.

But the real greatness of Johann Sebastian Bach was his faith. Here was a man who, like Moses, had seen God face-to-face, and had led his people into a Promised Land—a land now richer in music and faith because he lived there.